W9-BLX-490

ILLINOIS CENTRAL COLLEGE
PS3515.E37F357
STACKS
Hemingway's hidden craft :

A12900 383456

PS   Oldsey, Bernard
3515   Stanley, 1923-
.E37
F357   Hemingway's hidden
          craft

DATE			

WITHDRAWN

I.C.C. LIBRARY

© THE BAKER & TAYLOR CO

Hemingway's Hidden Craft

The Writing of *A Farewell to Arms*

Hemingway's Hidden Craft

The Writing of *A Farewell to Arms*

Bernard Oldsey

The Pennsylvania State University Press
University Park and London

I.C.C. LIBRARY   23998

Photographs courtesy of the John F. Kennedy Library

Library of Congress Cataloging in Publication Data

Oldsey, Bernard Stanley, 1923–
Hemingway's hidden craft.

Includes index.
1. Hemingway, Ernest, 1899–1961. A farewell to
arms. 2. Hemingway, Ernest, 1899–1961—Technique.
I. Title.
PS3515.E37F357   813'.5'2   79–743
ISBN 0–271–00213–1

Copyright © 1979 The Pennsylvania State University
All rights reserved
Designed by Glenn Ruby
Printed in the United States of America

For my wife, Ann;
my daughter, Jan;
and my son, Bill

Contents

Preface

The author is dead and we have all grown older but *A Farewell to Arms* remains print-fresh and alive in the collective imagination. This study of the inception and development of the novel marks the fiftieth anniversary of its publication. During a half-century of existence it has never been out of style, never needed any critical revival. Hemingway's tale of star-crossed lovers in wartime has established itself in the canon of modern literary art.

Like all such works of art it is sustained by the initiating and hidden acts of the craftsman. The present study attempts to reveal some of the methods by which the novel was composed, the raw materials out of which it was composed, and to some extent the literary structure into which it was composed. The underlying assumption here is that the close examination of the writing of one truly worthwhile novel can reveal something about the nature of all worthwhile novels. William Blake, after all, thought he could see the universe in a star, eternity in a grain of sand. And Jorge Luis Borges, in one of his essays, says that he might be able to comprehend everything about a given culture could he but read and thoroughly understand just one page of its writing.

This study is less sweeping in scope. As an examination of literary selectivity, it is offered as a contribution toward a definitive textual analysis of *A Farewell to Arms,* which can be attempted only when all the pertinent manuscript materials are made available for presentation in variorum format. The analysis begins with the problems inherent in the selection of thematic titles (Chapter 1); moves to the sliding relationship existing between autobiography and fiction (Chapter 2); and then proceeds to a consideration of two vital structural units of the novel—the beginning (Chapter 3) and the ending (Chapter 4). Perhaps more than any other compositional aspects of the novel, these last two, when closely examined, provide an expanded understanding and appreciation of the hidden craft of *A Farewell to Arms.*

Whatever merit this study may possess is due in considerable part to the generosity of Mary Hemingway, who allowed me access to the Hemingway papers and the right to publish manuscript material that had never before appeared in print (see especially Appendixes A and B). I am also indebted to the John F. Kennedy Library, particularly to Jo August, Curator of the Hemingway Collection, and to archivist E. William Johnson. I wish to thank my colleagues Joseph Browne, John P. Kent, Claude Hunsberger, Harry Marks, and David McKenty for various suggestions and comments pertaining to this work. For critical readings of the manuscript, I am particularly indebted to Carlos Baker, Charles W. Mann, and Philip Young, who, although not responsible for any errors that may have crept into the final version, helped eradicate earlier mistakes.

Portions of this study have appeared in *Modern Fiction Studies* and *Studies in American Fiction;* in altered form, they appear here by permission of these journals. Permission to quote from the published works of Ernest Hemingway is granted by Charles Scribner's Sons.

I would like to express my gratitude to West Chester State College for a travel grant that permitted me to work at the John F. Kennedy Library; and I would like finally to express special gratitude to my family for providing those emotive funds necessary to the completion of any literary task.

Bernard Oldsey
West Chester, Pa.

Introduction

"The Fine Times and the Bad Times"

Once a work of literature appears in print we tend to think of it as having come just that way, polished and complete, straight from the author's mind. Novels can create this impression as well as short stories and sonnets. In fact, the ability of certain novels to produce this effect may be an indication of their particular worth. A *Farewell to Arms* is that kind of novel, one whose art hides art. Its well-proportioned parts are arranged into five books nicely articulated to produce a series of dramatic climaxes leading to a tragic denouement. It can be read from cover to cover as a smooth chronicle of events that are so natural and real-seeming as to give some readers, even those with critical training, the idea that the novel is merely the outpouring of Ernest Hemingway's personal experiences in World War I.

Such a misconception does a disservice to the book and the reader, preventing the appreciation of an artistic effect and the perception of a critical truth. To understand and appreciate *A Farewell to Arms* as it deserves, we should examine some of the underlying acts of craftsmanship responsible for its finely wrought surface and resonant quality. When an examination of this kind is attempted—especially with the aid of the manuscripts housed in the John F. Kennedy Library—Hemingway's novel is revealed as a work of high creative order, the product of a series of drafts, rejections, recompositions, adjustments, and refinements. As subsequent chapters in this study indicate, Hemingway was, at least in this instance, the kind of writer he often said he was: one who wrote, re-wrote, and re-rewrote; who tested sentences for their shape, ring, and accuracy; and who worked hard to expunge the inevitable dross of composition from the final form. His drafts and emendations for this novel, his visions and revisions, add testimony to Yeats' dictum about writing: "It's certain there is no fine thing / Since Adam's fall but needs much laboring."

The labor began appropriately enough in Paris, city of many a writer's inspiration and deliverance. This is where Hemingway's art was developed, where his publishing began in small avantgarde presses, and where it all came to an end, in a sense, with the posthumous publication of *A Moveable Feast*, that tribute to the *panache* of The City of Light.

By 1927 Hemingway was established in Paris as an author of international repute, having by this time produced *Three Stories & Ten Poems, In Our Time, The Sun Also Rises, Torrents of Spring,* and a new collection of short stories, *Men Without Women.* He was no longer a foreign correspondent practicing the tricks of cable writing, nor a fledgling poetaster and short-storyist sitting at the pedagogical feet of Ezra Pound, Gertrude Stein, and Ford Madox Ford. He was now an accomplished writer who had developed a prose style of his own and had attracted a large following of devoted readers, including F. Scott Fitzgerald (who helped him jump from Boni & Liveright to the more prestigious publishing firm of Charles Scribner's Sons), as well as Malcolm Cowley and Edmund Wilson (whose early reviews helped establish and sustain his reputation).

By 1927 also Hemingway had acquired a new wife—after a separation from Hadley Richardson that proved so painful that he considered suicide as a solution even this early in life. Instead, he assigned all the royalties from *The Sun Also Rises* to Hadley and then married Pauline Pfeiffer, settling for a time in Paris. There, early in 1928, he started a new literary project, and in doing so abandoned a work in progress that had grown to about 40,000 words (it was to have been, as he informed editor Maxwell Perkins, the story of "a kind of modern Tom Jones"). According to Carlos Baker and Michael Reynolds, the new work began as nothing more than a short story, but as we shall see, the earliest manuscripts pertaining to it, among those preserved in the Hemingway Collection, are two linked chapters that seem to be the original beginning of *A Farewell to Arms*. [1]

This new narrative—which had as its first working titles *The World's Room* and *Nights and Forever*— took a little over a year to complete. In an introduction he did for the 1948 illustrated edition, Hemingway says that he began writing the novel in Paris and continued the work in such far-flung places as Key West, Florida; Piggott, Arkansas; Kansas City, Missouri; and Sheridan, Wyoming. He started writing "in the first winter months of 1928," and finished the first draft of the book in September of that year; he then rewrote during the fall and winter of 1928 in Key West and, coming full circle, did the final revisions in the spring of 1929 in Paris.

This period in Hemingway's life, just before and during the time of composition, was not only peripatetic but seemingly fated. Beginning with the divorce, tragic and near-tragic events so dominated his existence as to shatter any picture we might have of the novelist holed up somewhere tranquilly engaging his muse. The painfulness began on a side trip to Montreux, where Hemingway's son by his first wife poked a finger into one of his father's eyes, lacerating the pupil and for a while endangering sight (at this time Hemingway wrote to commiserate with the semiblind James Joyce about the difficulties of working with impaired vision). A month later, as accident prone as he was to prove all of his life, Hemingway suffered the singular misfortune of having a skylight in his Paris apartment fall on him—"gouging his forehead two inches above his right eye," as Carlos Baker informs us, "and felling him like a poleaxed steer." Ezra Pound wrote to Hemingway and asked how he had gotten "drunk enough to fall upwards thru the blithering skylight!"[2]

In the spring of that year, with Pauline pregnant, the Hemingways returned to the United States for the delivery of their child. They visited in Piggott for a while and then arrived in Kansas City just in time for Ernest to look in on the Republican National Convention (June 1928) that nominated Herbert Hoover for the presidency. Pauline's pregnancy was extremely difficult and pro-

3

tracted, ending with a Caesarean-section delivery of a son. Later that summer Pauline went off to join Ernest in Sheridan, Wyoming, where he was putting the finishing touches to the first draft of the novel, with Catherine Barkley, its heroine, about to die, after a Caesarean operation, in a Montreux hospital. That fall, after a duty visit to Oak Park, Illinois, where Ernest found his father ill and depressed, the Hemingways headed south and settled for a time in Key West. In December Ernest took a trip to New York and was on a train headed back to Florida when he received a telegram en route informing him his father had just committed suicide (December 6, 1928). He rerouted himself for Chicago and set off to help with the funeral arrangements.

Biographical notes like these might seem out of place in a study of the artistic fashioning of a novel, particularly a novel in which the author managed to transcend the level of fictionalized autobiography. But they point up one of the problems of composition and a concluding effect in *A Farewell to Arms*. As F. Scott Fitzgerald was to remind him, Hemingway had to face the fact that he was being prompted to write out of two sets of circumstances—the events and people associated with his war experiences in Italy (in 1918), and certain attitudes and emotions connected with this period of novelistic composition (1928–1929). In a footnote referring to the novel, Robert Penn Warren makes a similar point, although in listing contributing factors he fails to mention the suicide of Hemingway's father.[3] Hemingway himself was to refer openly to this matter in the short story "Fathers and Sons" and in *For Whom the Bell Tolls*. But there seems to be a hidden emotive trace of it also in the shocked conclusion of *A Farewell to Arms*, a trace made more noticeable by the funeral variants Hemingway wrote in trying to refine the conclusion of the book (see Chapter 4 and Appendix B of this study).[4]

During these months of constant travel and intermittent pain and pleasure Hemingway continued to work on the novel. "This was easier than it sounds," he tells us in an early handwritten version of the 1948 introduction, "since I had no choice in the matter and was driven by a compulsion to write which was a

4

complete enslavement." In a later typescript version of the introduction, he provides us with a fuller, more revealing view of the man and his work:

> I remember all of these things happening and all the places we lived in and the fine times and the bad times we had in that year. But much more vividly I remember living in the book and making up what happened in it every day. Making the country and the people and the things that happened *I was happier than I had ever been.* Each day I read the book through from the beginning to the point where I went on writing and each day I stopped when I was going good and when I knew what would happen next.
>
> The fact the book was a tragic one did not make me unhappy since I believed that life was a tragedy and knew it could only have one end. But finding you were able to make something up; to create truly enough so that it made you happy to read it; and to do this every day you worked was *something that gave a greater pleasure than any I had ever known. Beside it nothing else mattered.* [5]

The italicized phrases in these passages are strangely familiar to the Hemingway reader. Once they are associated with a story about a certain Francis Macomber, we realize that Hemingway was here describing "the short happy life of the writer." This was the same writer who had been considering taking the title "Disorder and Early Sorrow" straight from Thomas Mann to use for his own novel, finally rejecting it, among others, for the one we know. The rejection remains significant, for if these were the worst of times for the writer (full of sorrow and disorder), they were also, with the aid of his writing, the best of times.

The pattern of pain and pleasure associated with the composition of *A Farewell to Arms* gave way to one of pleasure and annoyance as the manuscript neared publication. Friends like F. Scott Fitzgerald, John Dos Passos, and Allen Tate who were allowed to read the work in its early stages invariably praised it as a modern masterpiece. After two deliriously pleased readings of the manuscript, the inordinately formal Maxwell Perkins threw aside reserve and took to addressing Hemingway as "Dear Ernest" in correspondence. And on February 13, 1929, Perkins sent Ernest a telegram that contained much good news and only a small amount bad: WISH TO SERIALIZE   FIRST INSTALLMENT BEING SET WITH SOME BLANKS   MAY ASK OMISSION OF TWO OR THREE PASSAGES. . . .   PRICE PROPOSED SIXTEEN THOUSAND. . . .[6]

The good news was summed up in the last segment of the message quoted: Scribner's intended to pay a young American novelist, just turned thirty, the then unheard of sum of $16,000 for the serial rights to his novel. Their previous high payments, to Edith Wharton and to John Galsworthy, were nowhere near that figure. The bad news was incorporated in the phrases "set with some blanks" and "may ask omission of two or three passages." *Scribner's Magazine* was a family magazine with a reputation for good taste, and in keeping with the contemporary sense of decorum the editors believed it necessary to excise and tone down some elements of Hemingway's frank tale of love in war.

Initially Hemingway writhed under the editorial censorship. He argued for the retention of words like *bedpan* and the uses they might suggest; he replaced *that* word for sexual coupling with euphemisms (substituting for it the past participle *cooked* twelve times in one remarkable paragraph); he muttered final imprecations about certain editorial tamperings with his prose; and then finally made peace with the editorial will. *A Farewell to Arms* ran in six installments in *Scribner's Magazine* from May to October 1929. Or at least it ran everywhere else except in Boston, where it was immediately and predictably banned as being an immoral work.

The issue in which the novel began contained a photograph of Ernest: he wears a moustache, a ski cap, and what appears to be a frown anticipating public reaction. The editorial caption introducing the novel is an awkwardly worded note playing up the socially redemptive quality of the book:

> This is the first novel by Mr. Hemingway since the great success of "The Sun Also Rises." Most of the action takes place on the Italian front during the period of greatest disaster. It is a love-story woven

with such a picture of war as would discourage either victors or the conquered from that terrible solution of international troubles.[7]

Actually the book could not compare in depiction of antiwar horror with such works as Henri Barbusse's *Under Fire,* Andreas Latzko's *Men in War,* and Richard Aldington's *Death of a Hero.* But Scribner's needed something to offset the puritanical reaction they feared might set in; and while *A Farewell to Arms* ran between the magazine's covers, it was accompanied by such staunchly upright materials as "Man's Faith" by Bishop Fiske, "New Education for Women" by Clarence C. Little, and a discussion of "The Catholic Advantage."

The first book edition of *A Farewell to Arms* appeared on September 27, 1929, just before the final serial installment. The book enjoyed immediate popular and critical success. Scribner's reprinted it twice in September (obviously expecting even better results than were at first anticipated), once in October, and three times in November, when sales stood at 79,251 copies.[8] Although Hemingway feared the effect of the stock-market crash (October 29, 1929) on the sale of books, his work continued to be a best seller until July of 1930; and by July 10, 1961, it had sold nearly a million and a half copies.

Reviews of the novel were equally encouraging, although a minor novelist named Robert Herrick wrote one of the strangest attacks ever aimed at an American novel. Headed "What Is Dirt?" Herrick's review contains this memorable bomb of review-manship: "I must confess that I did not stay with the story beyond the Milan episodes and so am not qualified to say whether such a love 'conceived in the muck of war' finally evolved into something which I should call beauty. I had had enough of what Mr. Wister quite properly calls 'garbage,' in which Mr. Hemingway so often wraps his pearls." After confessing that the novel was too dirty for him to read more than half of, and after garbling Owen Wister's favorable comment on the book, Herrick concludes that there would have been no loss to the world if *A Farewell to Arms* had been fully suppressed by a censoring body.[9]

With few other exceptions, however, the reviews were "splendid," as Perkins cabled Hemingway in Paris. Clifton Fadiman, Malcolm Cowley, Percy Hutchinson, T. S. Matthews, among others writing for the major journals, were alike in their high praise of the novel. Even those who did not fall completely under the sway of Hemingway as spokesman for the younger generation were willing to admit that in this instance he had produced a splendid work. Chief among these was Henry Seidel Canby, who was in favor of censorship in principle, but who wrote a perceptive review of the novel for *Saturday Review of Literature* (October 12, 1929), which included this eloquent defense of its morality:

> "Farewell to Arms" is an erotic story, shocking to the cold, disturbing to the conventional who do not like to see mere impersonal amorousness lifted into a deep, fierce love, involving the best in both man and woman, without changing its dependence upon the senses, nor trafficking with social responsibility. It deals with life where the blood is running and the spirit active—that is enough for me. As for Hemingway's frankness of language, to object to it would be priggish. There is no decadence here, no overemphasis on the sexual as a philosophy.[10]

Given today's prevalent sexual mores and language standards, we might have difficulty understanding what all the fuss over *A Farewell to Arms* was about, or at least we might have difficulty explaining the matter to young readers. Now, of course, the socially redemptive qualities of Hemingway's work are apparent. If the novel were to be charged along those lines, it might be, as Bertrand Russell once suggested, that Hemingway is too conventional a writer. Nor does there any longer seem to be any political reason to ban the book—as Mussolini did in Italy because it supposedly insulted Italian military honor and might do damage to national morale.[11]

The major remaining questions about *A Farewell to Arms* are not so much social or moral, but textual and formalistic: questions about the selection and arrangements of materials, questions about the art of composition. In attempting to answer such questions we may be able to decide whether F. Scott Fitzgerald—who read the novel with the discerning eye of a fellow novelist, and wrote nine pages of extremely perceptive notes about its contents to the author—was correct in his final judgment of its literary worth. Fitzgerald's concluding note simply runs: "A beautiful book it is!"[12]

"I think it is a very good one indeed, though it is one of those titles that is better after you read the book than before. But even at first sight it is a fine title."

—Maxwell Perkins, in a letter to
Ernest Hemingway, February 27, 1929

"One cannot help thinking that 'A Farewell to Arms' is a symbolic title: that it is Hemingway's farewell to a period, an attitude, and perhaps to a method also. . . ."

—Malcolm Cowley, *New York Herald Tribune Books*, October 6, 1929

1

Titles, the Title

Criticism has largely ignored titles as a subject. There is no single source one can turn to for information about the art of entitling in general or of entitling novels in particular. But Kenneth Burke, in his *Philosophy of Literary Form*, provides some valuable, if tangential, insights into the nature of titles when he tries to reduce literature to its lowest common denominator, in proverbs. He sees proverbs as bare statements of theme and sharp points of effect: they are books written in a sentence, as books are the expansion of a sentence. Emanating from somatic sources (initially as grunts, groans, shrieks, smiles), all forms of literature change inner into outer gestures. Moreover, they "name situations" in life and provide "strategies" for dealing with those situations. Thus, as Burke sees it, literature is "equipment for living," which in its various guises consoles, exhorts, warns, titillates, ridicules, etc.[1]

Beyond the level of simple label—which is what *titulus* means basically—novelistic titles function much like proverbs. They name situations in life (*Of Human Bondage*, for example) and often signal strategies for dealing with those situations (*Look Homeward, Angel*) in both the compositional and social sense. Indeed, if a historical account of novelistic titles is ever attempted, it will have to indicate how titles progressed from the earliest days of the novel, when they merely identified a situation and perhaps a subgeneric *modus operandi*, to a time in the nineteenth and especially twentieth century, when they indicated strategies through the increased use of imagery, symbolism, and allusion. The progression will lead, in other words, from such picaresque identifications as *The Life of Lazarillo de Tormes, His Fortunes and Adversities*, such sentimental designations as

Pamela, or Virtue Rewarded, and such Gothic representations as *The Castle of Otranto* to the more significating titles brought on in part by the novel of manners, as exemplified by *Pride and Prejudice* and *Vanity Fair.* In the twentieth century novelistic titles have expanded their functions so that they now summarize a plot (*Death Comes for the Archbishop*), characterize the protagonist (*The Great Gatsby*), establish an atmosphere (*Light in August*), underline a theme (*The Catcher in the Rye*), or preview an allegorical technique (*Ship of Fools* and *The Floating Opera*).

How much purchase a novelist gets from a title depends upon his selective ability and upon his attitude toward literature and life. Without discussing specific instances of effectiveness, we can easily follow the increase of sophistication in this progression of American novelistic titles: *Main Street, The Young Manhood of Studs Lonigan, The Grapes of Wrath, All the King's Men,* and *The Sound and the Fury.* The last three obviously gain allusive force, taken as they are from "The Battle Hymn of the Republic," "The Rime of Humpty-Dumpty," and *Macbeth.* They are representative of the auctorial art of selecting and applying titles which flourished among American writers of the twenties and the thirties, particularly T. S. Eliot, Ezra Pound, Wallace Stevens, Eugene O'Neill, F. Scott Fitzgerald, William Faulkner, and Ernest Hemingway.

None of these was more ardent in the search for the *exact* title than Hemingway. Any study written on the subject will have to reserve a niche for him as a practitioner of allusion and implication. The title, for example, of his first book of fiction probably comes from a passage (later made infamous by Neville Chamberlain) in the *Book of Common Prayer:* "Grant us peace in our time, O Lord."[2] The ironic point, of course, is that all of the sketches and stories that comprise *In Our Time* revolve around the violence and destruction granted the world instead of peace.[3] The title of *The Sun Also Rises* has its source in the opening section of *Ecclesiastes* where the preacher describes how one generation forgets another, how winds and ocean currents return to their sources, how the sun sets and also rises, and how there is "nothing new under the sun." The preacher also describes how, despite the foolish actions of man, the earth abides forever, in something of an ecological and spiritual triumph. A reader aware of the corresponding referents can perceive the underlying sense of *Weltschmerz* pervading Hemingway's novel and fully appreciate his paean to nature's beauty and peace as experienced in the Spanish Pyrenees. Another title, *Across the River and Into the Trees*, is a slightly altered version of General Stonewall Jackson's dying words. Hemingway applies them to his fictionally demoted general, Colonel Cantwell, who like his Civil War counterpart is dying and worries about how and where he will be buried. Of course, the most resonant of Hemingway's titles, *For Whom the Bell Tolls*, is a direct quotation from John Donne's famous Devotion XVII, which announces that "no man is an island" and that each man's death "diminishes mankind." As tolled by Hemingway, the bell announced that Spain was dying, along with freedom, and we did not have to send far to know that it was tolling for us and for others.

These four novelistic examples indicate how Hemingway states a literary theme and modality in titular fashion. Each title is the message of the work writ small (and, incidentally, it is difficult to understand why the British continue to publish *The Sun Also Rises* under its working label of *Fiesta*). Almost as important, however, these four examples reveal Hemingway's tendency to prefer titles that fall into two sometimes overlapping categories: (1) those that have topographical and / or climatological reference (like "Big Two-Hearted River," "Hills Like White Elephants," "The Snows of Kilimanjaro," "Cat in the Rain"); and (2) those that have religious and / or literary reference (like "The Light of the World," "Now I Lay Me," "Fathers and Sons," "In Another Country").[4] These and other peculiarities of taste and predilection reveal themselves in Hemingway's search for a title to a novel which he first called *The World's Room* and *Nights and Forever* before he settled on *A Farewell to Arms*.[5]

II

In his *Paris Review* interview with Hemingway, George Plimpton asked whether titles came to him while he was involved "in the process of doing a story." Hemingway replied, "No. I make a list of titles after I've finished the story or book—sometimes as many as 100. Then I start eliminating them, sometimes all of them."[6] Like a number of Hemingway's slightly bravura responses, this one is both informative and inaccurate and may lead, as this led Michael Reynolds, to an incorrect critical position.[7] The inaccuracy of Hemingway's statement becomes immediately manifest when we realize that just before embarking on *A Farewell to Arms* he started and never finished a novel which, nevertheless, he entitled *Along With Youth,* and even earlier than that had started another novel which he never finished (about one "Jimmy Breen") but which he entitled *A New Slain Knight.*[8]

The Hemingway papers show that he often used working titles for a novel in progress, and that he sometimes made lists of titles while in the process of finishing off a work, during the long and thorough revision period of composition. Apparently this is what happened with *A Farewell to Arms.* Hemingway began writing the novel in Paris in March 1928; he wrote most of the initial holograph version from April to July of that year (in Key West, Florida; Piggott, Arkansas; and Kansas City, Missouri); and then finished this version of the novel in August 1928 in Sheridan, Wyoming. It was not until nine months later, however, that the novel was put into final form; during the intervening period Hemingway did considerable revision, including typescript and galley changes.[9] The two earliest titles connected with the book appear on the cover of a composition tablet in handwritten form: *The World's Room* and *Nights and Forever.* They turn up again on a typed sheet inserted into the manuscript, along with two other possibilities: *The Hill of Heaven* and *A Separate Peace.* Finally, on two pages from a composition tablet, one full

Education of the Flesh.
The Carnal Education
The Sentimental Education
of Frederick Henry

Here is one General Guide
Pamphlet Without Desire
A World To See

Patriotic Prayers
The Grand Tour
The Italian Journey
The Wreck's Review
Disorder and Early Sorrow
An Italian Chronicle
The Time Exchanged
Death over Dead
They who I't slept.

The Italian Experience

Love In Italy
love In War.

I Have Committed Fornication
But that was In another country
and besides the wench is dead.

The Sentimental Education

Love In War
Sorrow For Pleasure
A Farewell To Arms

Idle Wisdom
The Enchantment

If You Must have
Wored Enough and Time
In Praise of His Mistress

Every Night and Day
Of Wounds And other Causes.
The Retreat From Italy.

AS OTHERS ARE

Hemingway's notes on the title.

sheet, Hemingway wrote a list of thirty possible titles, including *A Farewell to Arms*. Some of these are hand printed, some are written in cursive script: it is impossible to say whether the list was composed in one sitting or thirty. We cannot tell exactly when Hemingway decided upon *A Farewell to Arms* as the title; the earliest indication comes in December 1928.[10]

Since all of these titles indicate thematic thrusts and narrative emphases which Hemingway considered during the composition and revision of the novel, his handwritten list of possible titles is reproduced here in as close an approximation of their original order as possible:

Love is ane fervent fire
Kindlit without desire

> The source is Alexander Scott's "Rondel of Love" (c. 1530), p. 71 in the 1912 edition of *The Oxford Book of Verse*. Hemingway gave no indication how much of this he intended for a title. The theme of this poem—the hurtful uselessness of love—fits Hemingway's "In Another Country" even better than the novel.

A World to See

> From "A Praise of His Lady," anonymous, though possibly John Heywood's, pp. 82–84 *OBV*. Pertinent passage: "O Lord! it is a world to see" how virtuous and beautiful is the titular lady.

Patriots Progress

> A modification of John Bunyan's *Pilgrim's Progress*, 1678 [sic *Patriots*].

The Grand Tour

> With reference to the educational values of touring the major countries of Europe, including Italy of course.

The Italian Journey

> See above. [Hemingway's underline. This is also the title of Goethe's travel book *Italienreise.*]

The World's Room

> This was probably the leading choice for a title through most of the composition of the novel: it appears on a tablet cover, in a short typed list of four possibilities, and here in this list of thirty. It comes from the famous ballad "Edward, Edward," pp. 425–427 *OBV,* and is rather bitter in meaning: "The Warld's room" is what the young man will leave his wife and children, since he will never more see them.

Disorder and Early Sorrow

> Direct borrowing from Thomas Mann's fine short story of that title, published in 1925, just three years before the writing of Hemingway's novel. It indicates a mood of sadness and gloom that came after World War I.

An Italian Chronicle

> Simply a geographical label.

The Time Exchanged

Death Once Dead

> Reynolds hazards a guess that this may have come from
> William Drummond's "Spring Bereaved" (c. 1630), pp.
> 247–248 *OBV*, particularly the line "But we, once dead,
> no more do see the sun." His suggestion of Donne's
> "Death be not proud" is less likely.

They Who Get Shot

> Probably an adaptation of the title to Leonid Andreev's
> play *He Who Gets Slapped* (1915).

The Italian Experience

> [Hemingway's underline]

Love in Italy

Love in War

> [Hemingway's underline]

Education of the Flesh

> This is one of four titles that Hemingway tried to fashion
> from Flaubert's *L'Education Sentimentale* (1869); along
> with the next two, it is inserted marginally.

The Carnal Education

> See above [inserted marginally].

The Sentimental Education
of Frederick Henry

> See above [inserted marginally]. Here *Frederick* is spelled
> the same way the name is spelled for Flaubert's apprentice

hero, Frederick Moreau, in English versions. It is *Frederic Henry* in the novel. (Hemingway wavered on the spelling; and of course it was *Frédéric* in the French version of Flaubert's work.)

I Have Committed Fornication But that was <u>In Another Country And Besides</u> the wench is dead.

> Although this is from Christopher Marlowe's *The Jew of Malta* (1590), chances are that Hemingway saw it in epigraphic form attached to T. S. Eliot's early poem "Portrait of a Lady" [Hemingway underlined all of the phrasing indicated].

The Sentimental Education

> This is the fourth Flaubertian entry, an exact translation of Flaubert's title [inserted marginally].

Love in War

> The second page of entries begins with this, a repetition without underline.

Sorrow for Pleasure

> In all probability from "Icarus," an anonymous poem (c. 1601), p. 93 *OBV*. Here Icarus mounts on wings of love and warns men against flying too high; otherwise "Blinded they into folly run and grief for pleasure take."

A Farewell to Arms

> From George Peele's *Polyhymnia* (1590); a section of poetry entitled "A Farewell to Arms" in the *OBV*, pp. 142–143. [Full discussion follows.]

Late Wisdom

From George Crabbe's poem of the same title, p. 557 *OBV*. The rather obvious burden of this poem is that we learn through hard, full experience. This is the first of three entries Hemingway designated marginally as "Shitty titles." [Hemingway's underline]

The Enchantment

The second "shitty" title, this was actually struck through, but can still be read [Hemingway's underline]. It comes directly from Thomas Otway's poem of the same title (c. 1675), p. 486 *OBV*. This poem speaks of the briefness of love and the coldness of the lady in question.

If You Must Love

The third "shitty" title, this comes from Elizabeth Barrett Browning's *Sonnets from the Portuguese,* iv, the opening lines of which run: "If thou must love me, let it be for naught/ Except for love's sake only," p. 798 *OBV*. It expresses a rather soupy love-for-love's-sake theme.

World Enough and Time

From the opening line of Marvell's "To his Coy Mistress," "Had we but world enough, and time," pp. 387–388 *OBV*. [Later used by Robert Penn Warren as title of a novel.]

In Praise of His Mistress

Suggested by Marvell's poem [Hemingway's underline], and perhaps "Praise of His Lady."

Every Night and All

> From the second line of "A Lyke-Wake Dirge," which
> begins "This ae nighte, This ae nighte, / *Every Nighte
> and Alle,*" pp. 443–444 *OBV.* This vigil for the dead has
> an "Everyman" moral of good deeds. [N.B. For some
> reason, Reynolds gives the right source, but an incorrect
> entry of "Every Day and All."]

Of Wounds and Other Causes

<u>The Retreat from Italy</u>

> This suggests both the Caporetto retreat and the escape
> to Switzerland. [Hemingway's underline]

<u>As Others Are</u>

> [Hemingway's underline]

The three other possible titles Hemingway considered[11] in
manuscript form are added here:

Nights and Forever

> Reynolds suggests this is taken from the same source as
> "Every Night and All"; that is, "A Lyke-Wake Dirge."
> See above.

The Hill of Heaven

> Probably from "The Daemon Lover," an anonymous bal-
> lad about a wife who flees Britain with her lover, for
> "Italie," which contains the lines "What hills are yon,
> yon pleasant hills, / The sun shines sweetly on?" / "O

yon are the hills o' Heaven. . . ." They never reach them.

A Separate Peace

> This comes from Hemingway's own "Chapter VI" in *In Our Time* and will be discussed fully within the text. [Later used as a title for a novel by John Knowles.]

With minor variations, including slight errors in spelling and order, as well as one incorrect entry ("Every Day and All"), Michael Reynolds presents these titles in *Hemingway's First War*. The errors are minor, and by contrast the work he has done in searching out title sources is excellent. But his attitude toward the critical utilization of title information is strangely forbidding and negating: ". . . readers should not place undue emphasis on the novel's title, nor rely on the title's source as any sort of thematic key to its content. One must keep in mind that by 1929 the exegetical game had not yet begun in earnest, and Hemingway was not choosing a title with academic critics in mind." This punning caveat is preceded by an even more deadening pronouncement: "Neither the rejected titles nor the final title had any influence on the writing of the novel."[12] Reynolds here falls victim to the Pure Scholarship Fallacy. If the titles tell us so little about the themes, content, and composition of *A Farewell to Arms*, why bother to search out their sources so assiduously, or indeed list them at all?

Actually, the titles under consideration, as well as their sources, had considerable influence on the making of the novel. As we shall see more fully later, Hemingway tried in various ways to key sections of the novel to title possibilities and their sources. (The most obvious immediate example is his repeated reference and allusion in the text to Andrew Marvell's "To His Coy Mistress.") As for Hemingway's audience, by the time *A Farewell to Arms* was published, it included the likes of Ezra Pound, T. S. Eliot,

James Joyce, Gertrude Stein, Ford Madox Ford, Edmund Wilson, and Malcolm Cowley. An inner audience of this kind might be considered as capable as any academic exegetes in understanding and appreciating titular nuance. After all, nonacademicians Maxwell Perkins and Malcolm Cowley were among the first to declare *A Farewell to Arms* a "fine" and "symbolic" title.

The Hemingway papers provide us an unusual opportunity to study the relationship between a title, or titles, and a novel. There is no reason to shy away from two critical questions that arise quite naturally from scholarly information in this instance: (1) What do the projected titles tell us about the composition of the novel, including its thematic impulses? (2) What is so significant and appropriate about *A Farewell to Arms* that Hemingway chose it from among thirty-three carefully considered possibilities as the eventual designation of his book?

III

For this novel Hemingway searched almost exclusively among literary sources for his title. Only a handful of the thirty-three possibilities listed do not have literary bases; and those few that do not—like *Love in War* and *Love in Italy*—are rather flat, simple labels. Moreover, although he did look elsewhere, Hemingway concentrated his search to an unusual degree upon one source: almost half of the projected titles, fifteen, come from *The Oxford Book of English Verse.* [13] It is now apparent that Hemingway adopted this famous anthology—first published in 1900, under the editorship of Arthur Quiller-Couch—as something of a text and source book. Even before *A Farewell to Arms,* while working on the abortive novel about Jimmy Breen, Hemingway derived the tentative title *A New Slain Knight* from "The Twa Corbies," which appears in the collection. And sometime during the composition of *A Farewell to Arms,* he became enamored of another of its selections—the anonymous lyric "The Lover in Winter Plainteth for the Spring"—and from it fashioned a tender prose parody that occupies a vital position in the novel.[14] This extraction acts as a clue to Hemingway's thematic intention, because it emphasizes a further narrowing of selectivity in titles: in working through *The Oxford Book of English Verse*, Hemingway took all fifteen of his possibilities from ballads and love songs, particularly the courtly lyrics of the English Renaissance. One of these, although it had been first published in 1590 under the simple designation of "Sonet," as attached to George Peele's *Polyhymnia*, was an eighteen-line poem which Quiller-Couch represented in his anthology as "A Farewell to Arms."[15]

Hemingway's choices of title sources outside the anthology are somewhat more eclectic; but they too reveal an important thematic pattern, one acting as a counterbalance to the love interest. Indicative are two modern sources: Thomas Mann's "Disorder and Early Sorrow," and, peculiarly enough, Hemingway's own *In Our Time*. The Mann story had just been published, in 1925; and with its Teutonically clinical title, it stood forth as the historical epitome of the disillusionment that followed World War I. It indicated a social and intellectual wound that was the counterpart of what Hemingway was thinking about in listing such titles as *They Who Get Shot* and *Of Wounds and Other Causes*. But the Mann designation, appropriate as it might be for Hemingway's new novel, was too directly borrowed, too recently used for the original story (unlike Turgenev's *Torrents of Spring* and *Fathers and Sons*, which Hemingway did appropriate directly for a short novel and story). As for *A Separate Peace*, which comes from "Chapter VI" of *In Our Time*, it too represents wounds and late wisdom derived from the experience of war. But in this instance, as Reynolds suggests, the phrase contains an unwanted pun that Hemingway might not have wanted applied to Catherine Barkley.[16] Rejected as a title, the phrase "a separate peace" appears in the text of the novel, in a crucial selection of the action, and underlines the educative process that Frederic Henry goes through.

Even more heavily indicative of this process, the *Bildungsroman* aspect of the novel, are the title possibilities Hemingway took from John Bunyan and Gustave Flaubert. *Patriots Progress* — as Hemingway spelled this adaptation of *Pilgrim's Progress*— might very well have been an appropriate title for the novel, except that it leaves out the idea of romantic love. The possibilities derived from Flaubert's *L'Education Sentimentale* were capable of indicating various forms of love. Hemingway listed four titles based on this source, including again a direct borrowing. In all probability, he wanted to retain something of the French original in sense as well as phrasing: often "a sentimental education" in French connotes the amorous training provided a young man by a woman, often an older woman. Hence *The Carnal Education* and *Education of the Flesh,* as well as *The Sentimental Education of Frederick Henry.* (As noted earlier, Hemingway and Hemingway scholars have had trouble keeping the first name of the protagonist straight. Here in the title listings it is spelled *Frederick*; in the novel it is actually *Frederic.* Perhaps only coincidentally the name of Flaubert's protagonist in *L'Education Sentimentale* is Frédéric Moreau.)

A second piece of carnal education is indicated by another projected title, one of the most interesting and, as will be seen later, most important of the rejected possibilities. Peculiarly, Hemingway had already used it, or part of it, as title for the short story "In Another Country," published in April of 1927. If his underline on the holograph sheet of titles is truly indicative, he intended using the open-ended phrase *In Another Country And Besides* as the novel's full title. The phrase comes originally from Christopher Marlowe's *The Jew of Malta* (IV. 1, lines 42–44), where it has little or none of the "sentimental education" meaning attached to it in modern times. The probability is that Hemingway never read the play (he does not quote the dialogue correctly on his sheet), but that he came across the lines in the epigraph attached to T. S. Eliot's early poem "Portrait of a Lady" (1910). Eliot plays off the ironic Marlovian lines against the Jamesian contents of his poem in a manner that was not lost, inner pun and all, on his contemporaries.[17]

The identifying phrase "In Another Country" proves to be a

very special case in point. For one thing, it indicates that Hemingway learned, as a number of critics maintain, how to use titles of this kind from contemporaries like Ezra Pound and T. S. Eliot, who were intent on restoring allusion to full literary practice—not simply as decoration, but as a means of achieving resonance, depth, layers of sometimes contradictory meaning. For another, it indicates that Hemingway was especially attracted to the ironic tension in Marlowe's lines, especially for a work that was to be "a portrait of a lady," or that was to be written "in praise of his mistress." According to Carlos Baker, the attraction was present from the very beginning of *A Farewell to Arms,* as it was being conceived *ab ovo:*

> He had begun it early in March. . . . At first he had thought of it only as a short story like "In Another Country." He had been trying for years to make fictional use of his war experiences of 1918. He wanted to tell a story of love and war, using as an epigraph the cynical lines from Marlowe: ". . . but that was in another country, / and besides the wench is dead." The other country could only be Italia, and the girl Agnes von Kurowsky. She was neither a "wench" nor was she dead. But the story ached to be told.[18]

The thematic connection between the short story called "In Another Country" and the novel finally called *A Farewell to Arms* will be examined in the next chapter of this study; but there are a number of other connections between titles and works that should be mentioned here. Peculiarly enough, when the novel was published in Germany (1957) it appeared, presumably with Hemingway's approval, under the title of *In einem andern Land (In Another Country).*[19] And when the novel was banned in Boston during its serial publication (1929), Hemingway struck a doubly allusive note in referring to the book as "my long tale of transalpine *fornication* including the entire war in Italy and so to BED."[20]

As chance would have it, the two titles are even linked historically: Marlowe's *Jew of Malta* appeared, as the date is usually given, circa 1590; and George Peele's poem "A Farewell to Arms," or the poem so called and so attributed, was published in 1590. It was attached to his *Polyhymnia*—a blank-verse commemoration of the tournament held before Queen Elizabeth on her birthday that year. The original "A Farewell to Arms" depicts the withdrawal of Sir Henry Lee (destined by strange literary karma to become Lieutenant Henry?). Sir Henry was an actual person who, having grown too old to serve as Queen's Champion in the tournaments, requested upon this occasion that the Earl of Cumberland succeed him in this official post.[21]

In terms of literary analysis, the relationship between the Peele poem and Hemingway's novel is not so significant as that, for instance, between the Homeric epic and Joyce's *Ulysses*. But if we want to establish meaningful bases of understanding for Fitzgerald's *Tender is the Night* and Faulkner's *The Bear*, we had better have two of Keats' poems well in mind, since, respectively, "Ode to a Nightingale" and "Ode on a Grecian Urn" provide these two novels with contrapuntal subtlety and depth. And for the same reason the reader of Hemingway's "transalpine tale" of a modern knight, whose lust turns to romance, and whose romance turns to dust, should have before the mind's eye Peele's original version of the mustering-out process, reproduced here:

A Farewell to Arms
(To Queen Elizabeth)

His golden locks Time hath to silver turn'd;
    O Time too swift, O swiftness never ceasing!
His youth 'gainst time and age hath ever spurn'd,
    But spurn'd in vain; youth waneth by increasing:
Beauty, strength, youth, are flowers but fading seen;
Duty, faith, love, are roots, and ever green.

His helmet now shall make a hive for bees;
    And, lovers' sonnets turn'd to holy psalms,
A man-at-arms must now serve on his knees,

And feed on prayers, which are Age his alms:
But though from court to cottage he depart,
His Saint is sure of his unspotted heart.

And when he saddest sits in homely cell,
    He'll teach his swains this carol for a song,—
'Blest be the hearts that wish my sovereign well,
    Curst be the souls that think her any wrong.'
Goddess, allow this agèd man his right
To be your beadsman now that was your knight.[22]

It is impossible to say when Hemingway placed *A Farewell to Arms* on his list of possibilities or exactly when he decided on it as the title for the novel. According to Carlos Baker, however, Hemingway told his family, presumably in December of 1928, "that he had lately borrowed its title from that of a poem of George Peele's in *The Oxford Book of English Verse.*"[23] In all probability, then, it was not a seminal title out of which the entire book grew, having none of the early status of *The World's Room*, or *In Another Country*. Nor does it appear within the novel itself, directly or allusively, except as a synonymous echo of "a separate peace."

But Hemingway had this title in mind during a vital period of revision, including the remarkable conclusion which corresponds directly with the title; and he obviously chose it with great care from among a number of possibilities that might have done well, but not as well, in providing a key to, and a reinforcement of, the dominant themes and motifs of the novel.[24] The key, to novel or house, may be produced before, during, or after construction. There can be little doubt, after a study of the other possibilities and the allusive sources they represent, that Hemingway produced the right titular key at the right time—for the poem and the novel fit each other in a number of corresponding ways.

First, they both deal with that passage of time which changes youth into some form of agedness (the transition is mainly chronological in the poem, experiential in the novel; and it is difficult to decide which work contains a more advanced stage of world-weariness). Second, they both depict members of the military who take leave of military pursuits, seek peaceful refuge, and turn to prayer in service of their respective ladies. Peele's champion will now live in "homely cell," there to become a "beadsman," or teller of rosary beads, who lives "on prayer." In Switzerland, after deserting from the military, Lieutenant Henry becomes something of a modern beadsman, praying for Catherine Barkley in this realistically repetitious fashion: "Oh, God, please don't let her die. I'll do anything. . . . Please, please, please, dear God, don't let her die. Dear God, don't let her die. . . . I'll do anything you say if you don't let her die. . . ."

Third, and most important—for it is here that poem and novel reflect each other most dramatically and informatively—the two works center on the efficacy of abstract values and human virtue. In positive fashion Peele speaks of "Duty, faith, love" as Platonic universals that remain "ever green." Hemingway seems to speak negatively of much these same abstract qualities in this well-known diatribe:

> I was always embarrassed by the words sacred, glorious, and sacrifice and the expression in vain. . . . I had seen nothing sacred, and the things that were glorious had no glory and the sacrifices were like the stockyards at Chicago if nothing was done with the meat except to bury it. . . . Abstract words such as glory, honor, courage, or hallow were obscene beside the concrete names of villages . . . , the numbers of regiments and the dates.[25]

Probably the most famous passage in all of Hemingway's works, this may also be one of the best indicators of the inner tone and compositional method of *A Farewell to Arms*, but not for the reasons that seem most obvious. This passage is often discussed critically as an indication of thoroughgoing iconoclasm—and at first glance it appears to be nothing more than that. But it must be viewed in a literary context that goes beyond the novel itself. As T. S. Eliot maintains in his durable "Tradition and the Individual Talent," we must see a writer not only by himself but also in comparison with "the dead." Through this shifting process, we discover, as Eliot puts it, "the past [is] altered by the present as much as the present is directed by the past." Thus we cannot read an idealizing courtly-love poet like Peele as we once might have before the appearance of a pragmatic, realistic novelist like Hemingway. And much more important in this instance, we cannot read and truly understand Hemingway's *A Farewell to Arms* unless we consider how tradition, particularly that derived from English Renaissance poetry, gave it a new direction.

A clue to this influence can be found in Hemingway's vacillation between the harshly bitter lines of Marlowe and the adoring lyricism of Peele in choice of title, and really tonal effect. It would be wrong to view the eventual title as simply an ironic comment (like *In Our Time*) on all that romantic and religious poppycock. The tone of this novel (unlike that of *The Sun Also Rises*) is not that of the antiromantic, but that of the disappointed, or "ruined," romantic. It is the appropriate tone for a book that is presented as a battleground where we are privileged to view the immemorial struggle between man's idealization of the world and his reluctant acceptance of brute fact. That struggle is represented throughout the novel in oppositional pairs: (1) in Frederic Henry's enlistment in a noble cause, and his eventual desertion; (2) in Rinaldi's devotion to medical science, and his contraction of a venereal disease; (3) in the juxtaposition of the priest's good country of the Abruzzi, and the urban dens of iniquity Lieutenant Henry visits; (4) in the rear-echelon's patriotic view of combat, and the actual retreat at Caporetto; (5) in the idyllic love of Frederic and Catherine, and of love's labor lost in the still-born child; (6) in Catherine's warm womanly beauty, and her stone-cold corpse.

The rhetoric of event described here is antithetical, and it may seem as though brute fact demolishes romantic idealization in each instance. But there is a balance point, and if we look closely enough we can find it. Abstract words "such as glory, honor, courage" may be obscene, because they are deductive lies. Hemingway here proves to be an instinctive associate of the nominalist school of philosophers; that is, one who believes that there are no universal qualities in reality, and that abstract terms merely corrupt our thinking. But at the same time he also proves to be a celebrant of man's dignity, inductively arrived at, relative in nature, when he refers to "the concrete names of villages, the numbers of roads, the names of rivers, the numbers of regiments and the dates." Brute fact, when specified, can move in the direction of truth; times and places can register acts of courage and honor, but without the capital letters. This is what Hemingway more than implies when he writes that "only the names of places had dignity," along with "certain numbers" and "certain dates."

It is difficult, however, to keep inductive reason from becoming deductive: data are collected, observations made, and laws result. So Hemingway actually reinvests the old abstractions and the old romanticism with new meaning, by first resorting to partial iconoclasm. And in this pursuit he employs the title of *A Farewell to Arms* as a multipurpose implement in shaping the thematic contours of the novel. The title, as every college student knows, says good-bye to military arms and to love's embrace.[26] It may indeed, as Malcolm Cowley asserts, have said good-bye to a period of existence, to the hypocrisy of a war mentality, which Robert Graves took his literary leave of with his book entitled *Goodbye to All That* (published the same year as *A Farewell to Arms*, 1929). But it is even subtler than that and leads to a fact that commentators have missed in respect to the basic dialectic of the novel: by moving from traditional romance through parody to synthesized tragedy, Hemingway succeeded in producing a new dimension in modern fiction.

Although several critics have dealt with Hemingway's more obvious parodies, perhaps not enough attention has been paid to his overall tendency toward parody. He had, of course, in *Torrents of Spring* broadly parodied Sherwood Anderson's simplistic style and his drift toward romantic sentimentality. He showed the same tendency in many of his early attempts at versification—including a brief piece called "Neo-Thomist Poem," which twisted the 23rd Psalm to read: "The Lord is my shepherd, I shall not / Want him for long."[27] In *Across the River and Into the Trees* he echoed François Villon's famous refrain *"Mais où sont les neiges d'antan?"* and supplied it with a cloacal answer: *"Dans le pissoir toute la chose comme ça. . . ."* [28] Other examples of this parodistic tendency abound in Hemingway's work. Some of them (like the pity-terror-irony refrain in *The Sun Also Rises*) seem clumsy, even juvenile. But when we encounter something like the parody of the Pater Noster and Ave Maria in "A Clean, Well-Lighted Place," we can see one of the true functions of parody in a serious work of literature. Through similar, although more diverse, means Hemingway changed the sentiment of Peele's "A Farewell to Arms" into a symbolic fusion of idyllic romance and realistic doom.

One final look at the novel may insure an understanding of the parody-derived meaning of both book and title. At the end of this story, as Marlowe would have it, the "wench" is dead and in another country, after fornication. But she has been sung to sleep in a manner that even George Peele might have approved. Once again Hemingway resorts to parody, but tender parody in this instance, as once again he took his basic material from a piece of English Renaissance poetry— the anonymous lyrical quatrain mentioned previously, "The Lover in Winter Plainteth for the Spring," which runs as follows:

> O western wind, when wilt thou blow
> That the small rain down can rain?
> Christ, that my love were in my arms
> And I in my bed again![29]

This lyric was printed—some ninety pages away from Peele's poem—in the versions of *The Oxford Book of English Verse* available to Hemingway before 1929. From it, in describing Lieutenant Henry's state of mind during the wintry retreat from Caporetto, he produced this version of the lover's plaint:

Catherine was in bed now between two sheets, over her and under her. Which side did she sleep on? Maybe she wasn't asleep. Maybe she was lying thinking about me. Blow, blow, ye western wind. Well, it blew and it wasn't the small rain but the big rain down that rained. . . . Look at it. Christ, that my love were in my arms and I in my bed again. That my love Catherine. That my sweet love Catherine down might rain. Blow her again to me. . . .[30]

It is clear that this lyric and Peele's "A Farewell to Arms" worked their influence (along with the sources of such considered titles as *Every Night and All, Nights and Forever,* and *In Praise of His Mistress*) on the final shaping of *A Farewell to Arms.* Such evidence is certainly not enough to make anyone claim Lieutenant Henry to be the new Knight of La Mancha and Catherine the new Dulcinea. But it does signify an incorporating tradition of the novel. From one point of view—which entails knowledge of a romantic, chivalric past, and its uses within a medium combining parody and idealizing love—Hemingway achieved with *A Farewell to Arms* something distantly akin to Cervantes' *Don Quixote.* The one work is realistic, the other satiric. But both of these novelists, who were wounded out of combat, prove to be ruined romantics who, in a violent world they never made, artistically wished things could go better than brute fact allows.

IV

As Ernst Haeckel's famous line runs, "Ontogeny recapitulates phylogeny." So too Hemingway's projected titles for this novel recapitulate almost all of the various kinds of titles used for novels since the genre began: some are merely labels (like *Love in Italy*), some name a main action (like *The Retreat from Italy*), some bespeak the hard times undergone by the protagonist (like *Of Wounds and Other Causes*). But most are highly allusive and symbolic; they name situations in life and recommend strategies (like *If You Must Love*).

All thirty-three of the projected titles fall into somewhat overlapping categories: those pertaining mainly to war, to love, and to the education of the protagonist. *A Farewell to Arms* incorporates all three of these motifs, and resonates with allusive force. George Peele's "A Farewell to Arms" names the situation of the aged warrior who, idealizing his queen into a goddess, reluctantly leaves the field of honor. The concluding strategy implicit in his poem is that of prayer and poetry: the knight will become a beadsman, but he will also teach his swains to sing a certain carol in praise of his "goddess." Hemingway's title *A Farewell to Arms* names the situation of a young warrior who discovers that there is very little glory or honor on the field of battle, and that human love dies in the flesh. The strategy of this work is nevertheless somewhat like that of Peele's work: this young knight of "rueful countenance" will become a "wordsman," one who narrates the praises of his mistress in sometimes lyrical style, and enumerates with bitter irony the lessons of life that emanate from "wounds and other causes."

"Unlike many novels, none of the characters or
incidents in this book is imaginary. . . . The
writer has attempted to write an absolutely
true book to see whether the shape of a country
and the pattern of a month's action can, if truly
presented, compete with a work of the imagination."
— Foreword to *Green Hills of Africa,* 1935

"I remember living in the book and making up what
happened in it every day. Making the country and
the people and the things that happened I was
happier than I had ever been. . . ."
— Introduction to the illustrated edition of
A Farewell to Arms, 1948

From Autobiography to Fiction

The mystery of where autobiography leaves off and fiction begins has never been solved, and is perhaps insolvable. In one sense, every work of literature, no matter how imaginative, is autobiographic—to the extent that the writer does actually live out the composition of his work, which then stands as a record of the mental and even physical activity that went into its composition. In this sense, every writer "experiences" what he puts into his writing, no matter how "imaginary," "fantastic," or "exotic" that writing may be, and no matter how determinedly nonautobiographic the writer may want to be. Looked at from this point of view, Anatole France's *Penguin Island* is as autobiographic as D. H. Lawrence's *Sons and Lovers.*

This is not, however, the view we take of literature when we discuss its autobiographical content. Ordinarily the relationship between autobiography and fiction is analyzed on the basis of how much of the author's life, beyond his compositional activity, enters into the fictive work. We have in mind a sliding scale of contextual ratios: X amount of personal matter to Y amount of fiction. At one end of this scale we might place something like Joyce's *Portrait of the Artist as a Young Man* and at the other end something like H. G. Wells' *War of the Worlds.* Of course, the more realistic a novel is (like Joyce's), the more it tends to be autobiographical (or biographical); the less realistic (like Wells'), the less it tends to be so. As for subtypes of fiction, we find the *Bildungsroman* and the *roman à clef* quite naturally on the heavily autobiographic side, and the novel of fantasy and science fiction on the other. And in general, authors do not wander from one end of the scale to the other: Tolstoy stands here, Poe there.

Quite obviously Ernest Hemingway belongs on the mimetic, realistic, Tolstoyan side of this imaginary scale. That is to say, he belongs within the grand tradition of the novel that established itself within roughly a century, between 1830 and 1930— a tradition beginning with Balzac and including not only Flaubert and Zola but also the great Russian Realists, as well as James, Proust, Joyce, and Faulkner. Whatever differences exist among the works of these and related writers, they themselves were intent on depicting life with extraordinary verisimilitude, with concentration on some form of palpable, "historic" truth. The great bulk of their works would have to be placed near the center of the useful schema devised by Robert Scholes in his *Structuralism in Literature.* Flanked by romance and satire, "history" occupies a central position in this schema. Scholes represents literary modes taxonomically on the basis of whether they depict a world better than the one we think of as real, worse than it, or the equivalent of it. "Fiction," he declares, "can give us the degraded world of satire, the heroic world of romance, or the mimetic world of history."[1]

Again, the closer fiction comes to mimetic territory represented ideally as history (pure only in the ideal sense, since even history as written is contaminated by an auctorial personality), the more it tends to become biographical or autobiographical. And the critic who intends to make judgments about fiction on the basis of *its* purity—as Northrop Frye correctly indicates in his *Anatomy of Criticism*—is in for a difficult time. What are we to do with the personal-essay intrusions in *Tom Jones,* the historical dogma of *War and Peace,* the accounts of cetology in *Moby-Dick,* the auctorial self-analysis in *A la recherche du temps perdu*? Unless we are absolute Platonists we cannot insist that there is a single form which is *the* novel, and that the works just mentioned are "impure examples" which must be judged inferior works of art. And unless we are going to be biased in some other generic sense, we cannot denigrate fiction as being too autobiographic, or autobiography for being too fictional. If we behave this way, we will have difficulty reading, appreciating, and assessing any work that does not conform with preset genres, like the personal-essay *ficciónes* of Jorge Luis Borges and the so-called "nonfictional novel" as practiced by Truman Capote and Norman Mailer.

For several reasons, the critic who deals with Ernest Hemingway should keep all of these matters in perspective. One reason is that Hemingway has been charged with being "too autobiographical." Another is that he himself has had a few things to say about the intricate interaction between fiction and autobiography, and has produced works of varying nature in terms of this interaction. Still another reason, and the most important, is that *A Farewell to Arms* is an achieved fiction which emerges from an autobiographical past—experiences in love and war—that Hemingway refined through several stages of composition, including short stories that act as informing tributaries to the novel itself.

In all probability, the accusation that Hemingway's work is "too autobiographical" began with the publication of *The Sun Also Rises*. But the worldwide publicity given to his life, and his death, has helped make this charge increasingly pervasive and inclusive; and so have a number of ghoulish biographies, like A. E. Hotchner's *Papa Hemingway*, that treat his life as his work, and vice versa. These and certain *ad hominem* attacks, like Wilfrid Sheed's, recently published in *The New York Review of Books*,[2] have riddled the Hemingway corpus, savaging a dead member of the writing clan in perverted fashion. There is no denying that some of Hemingway's work does lend itself to the charge that it is egocentric and self-seeking; but such a charge applied indiscriminately to all of his work sinks to mere prejudice and interferes with clear critical judgment.

Across the River and Into the Trees, for example, is undeniably a bad novel, not because it contains too much personal material, but because it poses as a novel and is in reality just a weak *apologia*, a form of artistic untruth. The same thing could be said of *Islands in the Stream*, except of course that Hemingway himself was not responsible for the publication of this posthumous work.[3] But *The Sun Also Rises* is another matter. It too represents much personal experience and is in fact a thoroughgoing *roman à clef,* as evidenced fully in Bertram Sarason's collection of essays entitled *Hemingway and The Sun Set.* [4] A number of excellent works of fiction, however, qualify for the designation *roman à clef* and at the same time depend upon a protagonist based on the author—including Joyce's *Portrait of the Artist,* Lawrence's *Sons and Lovers,* and all of Proust's *A la recherche du temps perdu.* [5] Obviously, then, critical judgment must be determined by something other than simply the amount of autobiographical material utilized. It is necessary to ask how such material is used in the process of imagining, of combining and recombining, of refining within a fictive whole. It is also necessary to ask whether *The Sun Also Rises* belongs with the works just mentioned, or with those, say, of Henry Miller and Norman Mailer. The first category represents the highest kind of creative quality; the second, which includes *Across the River,* a shady area of undigested autobiography mingled with undistinguished fiction.

As stated previously, the interaction between autobiography and fiction is extraordinarily intricate. Lines of demarcation cannot be precisely fixed where realistic fiction, autobiographical fiction, fictionalized autobiography, and "straight" autobiography are concerned. They should be viewed, with constant critical adjustment and assessment, as interpenetrating elements arranged along a continuum. At times Hemingway himself sensed the intricacy of the problem, both for the writer and the reader. In the early 1930s he experimented with a form of fictionalized documentary and produced *Green Hills of Africa* (1935), which is a pioneer work of the kind now referred to as the "nonfiction novel." The techniques usually thought of as fictional—including scene, action, dialogue, scale, and narrative "persona"—are evident throughout the book. Hemingway's mode of narrative expression and his literary expectations are enunciated in his short foreword: "Unlike many novels, none of the characters or incidents in this book is imaginary. . . . The writer has attempted to write an absolutely true book to see whether the shape of a country and the pattern of a month's action can, if truly presented, compete with a work of the imagination." The use of the words "characters" and "pattern" indicates the overall attitude of the fiction writer. That attitude becomes involute in the note written as preface (in 1960) to *A Moveable Feast.* An admixture of nostalgia and satire, this late work of Hemingway's so defied his own powers of classification that it evoked this strangely elliptical advice: "If the reader prefers, this book may be regarded as fiction. But there is always the chance that such a book of fiction may throw some light on what has been written as fact."6

Green Hills of Africa and *A Moveable Feast* represent two different kinds of fictionalized autobiography: the first is more straightforwardly biographical, more objective and documentary; the second, as Hemingway's foreword indicates, moves under the controlling aegis of a narrating persona that is close to fictive. As already noted, *Across the River* and *The Sun Also Rises* represent two different grades of autobiographical fiction. *A Farewell to Arms* and *The Old Man and the Sea* are works of another order. Much less dependent upon personal experience than any of the previously mentioned works, these are both examples of highly realistic fiction. Each in its own distinct manner represents the kind of fiction Edmund Wilson said could be achieved by fusing naturalistic and symbolic methods. A preponderance of Hemingway's short stories fit within this class also—most remarkably stories like "A Clean, Well-Lighted Place" and "The Snows of Kilimanjaro." The critical point, then, is that Hemingway produced works of varying quality within all three of the fiction-autobiography areas mentioned. It is the discriminating reader's job to keep his works from being lumped together under one indiscriminate and pejorative heading.

This can be done if we understand the basic distinction between autobiography and fiction. Autobiography is related to history in that both are supposed to be narrative statements of fact, subject to corroborative or noncorroborative evidence. Both announce to the reader, or listener, that *this* is the truth. In actuality, however, autobiography is more closely related to history's dark shadow, propaganda. It is a form of public relations in which the author places himself in the position of telling the world the truth about himself—the truth as he sees it, or wants it to be seen. Hemingway came close to saying this in his advice to the reader of *A Moveable Feast,* which is public relations at its artistic best.

Fiction differs markedly from autobiography in attitude and aim. Like drama it asks for a suspension of disbelief, and thus from the outset announces that *"this* is not necessarily true." Like poetry it asks for a certain leeway or license, and thus admits that its contents will be governed by form and technique, either traditional or organic. Fiction sets out to lie (to "fabricate," as we say) in hopes of arriving at some form of inner truth, and sometimes even a transcendent truth. As a seer may use a trance, or a fool the cloak of foolery, the writer of fiction uses a mask from behind which he is free to utter the truth. Whatever the source of that truth (critics of religious, social, political, psychological, and semiotic bent all have their favorite concepts of source), it is produced through the artistic process. When achieved, such truth resides within the artistic construct, not within any espousing cause, not even the author. This is what D. H. Lawrence meant when he said, "Never trust the artist. Trust the tale. The proper function of a critic is to save the tale from the artist who created it."[7]

This critical separation of work from author was sought on more formal grounds by W. K. Wimsatt and Monroe C. Beardsley: in their well known essay on "The Intentional Fallacy" they argue "that the design or intention of the author is neither available nor desirable as a standard for judging the success of a work of literary art." But even during the heyday of New Criticism, Wimsatt and Beardsley avoided the pitfall of purism by admitting that "the use of biographical evidence need not involve intentionalism, because while it may be evidence of what the author intended, *it may also be evidence of the meaning of his words and the dramatic character of his utterances. "*[8] The last part of their statement should be stressed here in considering how elements of Hemingway's life enter into *A Farewell to Arms* and become transmuted, along with imaginative elements, into a form of art-truth. However, since Hemingway produced clusters of related fictions within a continuing *œuvre,* we should also observe how earlier fictional uses of autobiographical materials, which then reappear in *A Farewell to Arms,* contributed to the composition of the novel. For in this instance pieces of life and pieces of fiction reflect considerable light upon the completed artifact.

Such light is shed mainly upon three central aspects of the novel: the love affair, the wounding of the protagonist, and the catastrophic conclusion to idyllic love. To some extent these all came from the author's own experience, but to a much larger extent they are the product of creative imagination. Although it may be tempting to read Hemingway (or Joyce or Proust) from a strictly biographical viewpoint, doing so leads to critical perversion, to circular thinking of the worst kind. To avoid this kind of error, a simple setting forth of fact—as best we have it, mainly from Carlos Baker's painstaking biography—constitutes an analytical first step:

1. Hemingway volunteered for the Red Cross ambulance service in 1918; he was accepted in May, given the honorary rank of second lieutenant, and sailed for Europe May 21.

2. He was assigned to American Red Cross Section Four and sent to the Italian-Austrian front. There he drove ambulances for a short time near Schio in the Dolomites before taking charge of a Red Cross canteen near the front lines at Fossalta, a village north of Venice on the Piave River.

3. He was not a combat soldier in any sense; but he did come under fire in delivering materials to men in the front lines.

4. In the combat area for approximately a month, he was the first American wounded in Italy in World War I—sometime near midnight on July 8, 1918, about two weeks before his nineteenth birthday. He was at a forward listening post on the west bank of the Piave near Fossalta when a *Minenwerfer* shell wounded him. Carrying another wounded man, Hemingway made his way toward the rear and was hit again, this time by machine-gun fire.

5. He spent five days at a field hospital and had twenty-eight

Milan, Italy, 1918
Ernest Hemingway and Agnes von Kurowsky,
upon whom the character Catherine Barkley is partially based.

pieces of shrapnel removed from his legs and feet (about a hundred more could not be extracted). He was then shipped to Milan, where he was admitted to the Ospedale Croce Rossa Americana. By mid-August he had two machine-gun bullets removed from a foot and knee.

6. By mid-August also he was in love with an American nurse named Agnes von Kurowsky, a tall dark-haired young woman from Washington, D.C. So far as literary scholarship reveals, their five-month romance remained sexually unconsummated. It was interrupted by Agnes' reassignment during an influenza epidemic. Back at the front, Ernest discovered he had jaundice and returned immediately to the hospital in Milan. The pair were together again for a short time, then once more separated by her duties. Agnes' letters eventually advised Ernest to return to the United States. The romance ended rather bitterly on his part. He was nearly twenty at the time; Agnes was twenty-seven.

7. During his stay in Milan Hemingway was befriended by a lively young Italian captain named Enrico Serena, who took to calling him "Bambino." On a trip to Lago Maggiore with another wounded comrade, Hemingway was also befriended by Count Giuseppe Greppi, then ninety-eight years old, a former diplomat, who played billiards with him and treated him to champagne in the game room of the Gran Hotel Stresa.

8. Hemingway landed in New York on January 21, 1919, thus ending a nine-month tour of duty abroad.

Anyone reading this deliberately stringent chronicle can find in it the rites-of-passage elements that went into the making of a fine *Bildungsroman.* But these are raw materials. Anyone comparing them with their final development in *A Farewell to Arms* can see how art improves on life. Hemingway did *not* have the love-of-his-life affair that Lieutenant Henry does. He was *not* a combat hero, and did *not* shoot anyone. He was *not* involved in the Caporetto retreat. He did *not* desert criminally, if justifiably; and he did *not* flee to Switzerland. He was *not* the common-law husband of a beautiful Scotch woman, was *not* the father of her stillborn child.

To the initial set of facts, the determined literary and/or psychological analyst might want to add a second set pertaining to other experiences—from 1921 to 1929—that may have contributed to the composition and revision of *A Farewell to Arms:*

9. Hemingway married Hadley Richardson September 3, 1921; and, as correspondent for a Toronto newspaper, settled in Europe. In June 1922 he took his bride on a trip to visit the places he had been to in the war, including Milan, Schio, and Fossalta.

10. Their marriage deteriorated in 1926, and in January 1927 Hemingway divorced Hadley (the woman, according to his account in *A Moveable Feast,* he was to love for the rest of his life). In May 1927 he married Pauline Pfeiffer. At the time he considered himself a nominal Catholic (having been anointed by an Italian priest while being treated for his wounds in 1918).

11. In the mid-twenties, with Hadley and then with Pauline, Hemingway spent idyllic ski vacations in the Swiss Alps not far from Lake Geneva.

12. During the composition period of *A Farewell to Arms* Pauline suffered through an eighteen-hour ordeal (June 27–28, 1928) that ended with a Caesarean-section delivery of a son, Patrick.

13. During the revision period of the novel, Ernest's father, Dr. Clarence Hemingway, who had been ill and depressed for some time, committed suicide (December 6, 1928), shooting himself with a revolver.

These notes indicate that life can, directly and indirectly, provide elements for the thematic structuring of a novel like *A Farewell to Arms.* We can find in the notes the bases for such characters as Frederic, Catherine, Rinaldi (from Captain Serena), Count Greffi (from Count Greppi), the priest (from the anointing priest); and for such events as the wounding of Frederic, his treatment and love affair in Milan, the idyllic honeymoon in Switzerland, the Caesarean section performed on Catherine, and the remorseful conclusion of the novel (occasioned by the death of a loved one, Hemingway's father). But it is in the reshaping and ordering of such motivational factors, and in the addition of imaginative elements to them, that the realistic novelist achieves artistic primacy. A second look at notes and novel shows how Hemingway established this primacy in *A Farewell to Arms.*

In respect to characterization, he worked in much the same manner that representational muralists and sculptors do—utilizing models in direct, indirect, and composite fashion; but utilizing at the same time a structuring imagination to produce a realized form of art. Count Greppi exemplifies direct utilization: Hemingway used him almost as he did King Victor Emmanuel III, as an actual historical figure. He changed the circumstances of his meeting with Greppi in Stresa only slightly for an episode in the book (substituting Catherine Barkley for the actual wounded companion who accompanied him on the trip); and in fact he changed the Count's name, to *Greffi,* only after the book had been set in galleys. But major characters, like the priest and Captain Rinaldi, are fleshed out far beyond their simple biographical beginnings—Captain Serena, for example, being transformed into the medical officer Rinaldi, who is Lieutenant Henry's boon companion in the combat zone. And the character Catherine Barkley proves to be an even more complex matter—based as she is partly on Agnes von Kurowsky, partly on Hadley Richardson, partly on Pauline Pfeiffer; and then rounded into fictional fullness by the imagination and the demands of the novel.[9]

As for the war background, Michael Reynolds' excellent treatment of the extensive research that Hemingway did in writing the novel should silence adverse criticism stemming from the "too autobiographical" charge.[10] What Reynolds reveals is the fact that Hemingway, who was in the combat area only about a month, and who missed the first twelve battles of the Isonzo, and who had not even enlisted in the ambulance corps by the time the Caporetto retreat occurred, researched the war sections of his novel almost as thoroughly, and with as little previous knowledge of the pertinent events, as did Stephen Crane and Emile Zola in writing *The Red Badge of Courage* and *La Debâcle.* The Caporetto retreat section of the novel (Book Three) is so realistically and powerfully written that it was taken as gospel by some of those who had actually been part of that great disaster; and it was responsible for getting the novel banned in Italy by the Mussolini government, because it might be harmful to national pride. That section of the novel is a triumph of fictive imagination backed by research.

In other words, Hemingway found that "real life" would not do. Lieutenant Henry, who does take part in the Caporetto retreat, and who finds in it the reasons for his "separate peace," shares very little by way of war experiences with the author. Henry is wounded near Gorizia on the Isonzo River, near the present-day Italian-Yugoslav border in the Julian Alps; Hemingway never reached that front, but was wounded some forty or fifty miles to the west on an entirely different front at Fossalta on the Piave River. Lieutenant Henry is depicted as having been in the war from its beginning, for nearly four years (a factor contributing to his disillusion and "separate peace"); Hemingway was in the combat zone for only a few weeks, at a time when the Italian forces were getting ready for a push that was actually going to move the Austrian forces all the way back to the sector where the Caporetto retreat had begun, and indeed end the war in that region.[11]

II

Anyone comparing the biographical elements with their final disposition and imaginative development in *A Farewell to Arms* can see how literary art, even when highly "realistic," improves on life—the way, say, a painting by Whistler or Wyeth does. The truth is that for this novel Hemingway combined autobiography and research along with wish-fulfillment in the dramatic elaboration of an imaginary life. And he began this process of elaboration in a number of short fictional attempts that preceded the encompassing form of the novel. Examining these fictional stages serves two critical purposes: it provides a developmental context for reading discrete sketches and stories that are not best understood by themselves; and it provides a diagram of how these submaterials were transformed into a fully accomplished work of fiction.

There are five pieces written before the novel that contribute to an understanding of the eventual selectivity and motif-arrangement exercised in the making of *A Farewell to Arms.* Three of these were published in the 1924 and 1925 versions of *In Our Time.* "Chapter VI" of the latter version is a one-paragraph sketch that describes the first of Hemingway's woundings. Nick Adams, a prototypical protagonist who eventually shades into Frederic Henry, lies *hors de combat* in a sunlit Italian village, wounded in the spine. His wounded companion is named Rinaldi —an important name in the novel, although nothing in "Chapter VI" as yet indicates that this character is an officer and physician. More important than this truncated Rinaldi are the thematic units of antipatriotism and "a separate peace" which are first established here and indeed provide the sketch with its peculiarly satisfying conclusion. "Senta Rinaldi," Nick says, "You and me we've made a separate peace," and adds smilingly—"Not patriots." These elements are repeated several times in *A Farewell to Arms,* most notably in Lieutenant Henry's discussion with Gino (pp. 190–91) and during his escape from the front lines to Milan, when he declares, "I was going to forget the war. I had made a separate peace" (p. 252).

"Chapter VII," another one-paragraph sketch of war, stands as an early example of Hemingway's method of rubbing the sacred and the profane together to generate dramatic tension. The point of "Chapter VII" is that a man may require the Lord as his shepherd in combat, but may deny Him (neo-Thomistically) in a whorehouse. It opens "While the bombardment was knocking the trench to pieces at Fossalta," and depicts a soldier praying repetitively for his own life, as Lieutenant Henry later does for Catherine's. And like Lieutenant Henry, this soldier is a frequenter of those houses of prostitution referred to generically as the "Villa Rossa." It is in one of these, as the sketch closes, that he denies both the Lord and prayer: "The next night back at

Mestre he did not tell the girl he went upstairs with about Jesus. And he never told anybody."

Of course Hemingway told—and a number of times, because he had discovered the literary efficacy of mixing religion with mundane duress. As something of a Catholic *manqué*, he was basically a secular writer searching for religious significance. This tendency reveals itself in many of his works, including *The Sun Also Rises*, with its biblical title and Brett Ashley's concluding moral pronouncement: "It's sort of what we have instead of God." It shows up in stories like "Soldier's Home," where a returned veteran finds it impossible to pray, even though his mother cajoles him into kneeling by her side. But the tendency receives fullest expression in Hemingway's profane depiction of the Crucifixion, "Today is Friday." Through the kind of artistic freedom that would lead to *Jesus Christ Superstar*, this playlet, like Ezra Pound's "Ballad of the Goodly Fere," pictures Christ as a man among men, "no capon priest."

In *A Farewell to Arms* the sacred-profane motif is strongly developed along lines that parallel Henry's relationship with the priest. Appropriately enough—or inappropriately enough—we first see the priest from a whorehouse window, as Lieutenant Henry occupies one of the upper rooms with a "friend," watching the priest walk by in the initial snowfall of the year. Later we see him in the officers' mess, where he beseeches Lieutenant Henry to go to the clean, cold snowy region of the Abruzzi on his leave (Lieutenant Henry goes instead to more whoring spots in Rome, Florence, etc.). At mess, the priest is made a mockery of, especially sexually and politically. But he accepts the officers' cruel jibes, understanding that these are men who have been under great stress, and accepting their crown of barbed comments with the charity and equanimity of the Christ figure in "Today Is Friday." And eventually he succeeds—with some help later from Catherine Barkley and Count Greffi—in teaching Lieutenant Henry that the love of God and the love of a woman can be part of the same religion.

"A Very Short Story," so titled in the second version of *In Our*

Time, reads like one of Bret Harte's "Condensed Novels," cap-
ing as it does within its seven short paragraphs almost the ent__
scope of *A Farewell to Arms.* This harshly rendered "love story"
approaches the autobiographical much more than does the novel.
Here the protagonist, wounded in an unspecified manner, has
been sent to a hospital in Milan (changed to Padua in this version). He has a love affair with an American nurse named Ag
(changed to Luz, because the name of the actual girl was Agnes
von Kurowsky). Eventually the lovers are separated by the nurse's
duties, and the young man finally sails for home. There he receives letters in which she explains that she has fallen in love with
an Italian major who intends to marry her. All this so closely
parallels what actually happened to Hemingway that it is probably
fair to conclude that the ending of the story reflects the author's
own personal bitterness, if not spitefulness: "The major did not
marry her in the spring, or any other time. Luz never got an
answer to the letter to Chicago about it. A short time later he [the
jilted narrator] contracted gonorrhea from a sales girl in a loop
department store while riding in a taxicab through Lincoln Park."
There we have the truly antiromantic presentation of the love
theme, product of the hard-boiled school of writing. No doubt
Hemingway earned a diploma in that school; but all we need do
is compare this story with *A Farewell to Arms* to realize that he
also went on to graduate studies in variations on a theme and
fuller uses of the imagination.

"In Another Country" and "Now I Lay Me" are variations on
a theme at a more advanced stage of fictive development. Both
published in *Men Without Women* (1927), they deserve to be
read as companion pieces, reflecting as much light on each other
as they do subsequently on the novel. Both revolve around a
question that always seems topical and new and that nevertheless
plagued not only Pyramus and Thisbe, Romeo and Juliet, but
Ernest and Agnes, as well as Frederic and Catherine: To wed, or
not to wed?

The lesser of the two stories, "Now I Lay Me," seems, at least
on the surface, to advocate marriage—as a form of therapy for the

protagonist, Nick Adams again, who has been wounded and cannot sleep nights (hence the title from a child's bedtime prayer). The advocate of marriage is Nick's companion, an Italo-American named John, who tells him—"You ought to get married, Signor Tenente. Then you wouldn't worry. . . . You been wounded a couple times. . . . You ought to get married." In *A Farewell to Arms*, Lieutenant Henry himself argues the psychological advantages of marriage, formal or de facto as the case may be. He speaks for all those Hemingway heroes who are wounded, neurotic, insomniac, and afraid of the dark: "I know that the night is not the same as the day: that things are different . . . and the night can be a dreadful time for lonely people once their loneliness has started. But with Catherine there was almost no difference in the night *except that it was an even better time*" (p. 258, italics added).

Unfortunately for Nick Adams, he has no such companionship or love. As he lays himself down to sleep, listening for hours to silkworms gnawing mulberry leaves, he has to think of other things than either prayer or a woman's arms to achieve comfort or release. "Finally," he tells us, after considering John's marital advice, "I went trout-fishing, because I found I could remember all the streams . . . while the girls, after I had thought about them . . . blurred . . . and all rather became the same . . . and I gave up thinking about them altogether." Nick is truly one of the titular "men without women." He looks toward the therapy of nature advocated in "Big Two-Hearted River" rather than that of love advocated in *A Farewell to Arms*.

"In Another Country" asks the same question about marriage and does look toward the novel. This story turns on the sad predicament of an Italian major, a hero, a real "hunting hawk," who unlike the American narrator has truly earned his medals. The title of the story, as previously noted, refers to a young woman, or "wench," who is dead—in this instance the beautiful young girl whom the major marries only after he himself has been "safely invalided out of the war." Then fatal irony presses itself home, as the young wife dies from pneumonia shortly after their wedding.

One difficulty in trying to use "In Another Country" simply as a developmental marker is that it is itself a beautifully finished piece of fiction. Much of its polished effect proceeds from a well designed opening which—like the opening chapter in *A Farewell to Arms*—works on a climatological principle and functions as an overture to the entire work:

> It was cold in the fall in Milan and the dark came very early. Then the electric lights came on, and it was pleasant along the streets looking in the windows. There was much game hanging outside the shops, and the snow powdered in the fur of the foxes and the wind blew their tails. The deer hung stiff and heavy and empty, and small birds blew in the wind and the wind turned their feathers.

The deadly conclusion of *A Farewell to Arms* lies latent in the first chapter of the book. So, too, everything that occurs in "In Another Country" lies implicit in the opening passage quoted here: the dark has come early, for the young wife; there has been a form of hunting; the wounded men in the hospital are stiff and empty; and as the narrator confesses, he is one of the small birds, not a hunting hawk.

Much of this must be sensed if we are to understand the angry, bitter attitude of the Italian major. He replaces John as an advisor on the question of marriage. His answer is an equivalent of Francis Bacon's in his essay "Of Marriage and Single Life"—namely, "He that hath wife and children hath given hostages to fortune. . . ." When the American narrator, who as yet knows nothing of the major's misfortune, asks about marriage, he is unprepared for the vehemence of the answer: "He cannot marry. . . . If he is to lose everything, [a man] should not place himself in a position to lose that. . . . He should find things he cannot lose."

It is at this point that the experiences, tonalities, and themes of "In Another Country" and *A Farewell to Arms* cross and merge. The Italian major is in the same tragic situation as Lieutenant Henry at the conclusion of the novel. What becomes thematically clear in both works is that there can be no such thing as "a separate peace," because everything in life is battle (*"La vida es una lucha,"* as the Spanish proverb has it). There is no such thing as being "safely invalided"; and there is no place on earth —not Switzerland or any other supposed bastion of neutrality— where we can buttress out death and destruction.

Ultimately, then, *A Farewell to Arms* emerges as a culminating and rounded variation on themes stemming in part from the author's experience and developed piecemeal in five short works written before the novel. "Chapter VI," "Chapter VII," "A Very Short Story," "Now I Lay Me," and "In Another Country" helped develop such vital elements of the novel as these: (1) the initial wounding of the protagonist (who is then neurotic, insomniac, and in need of therapy); (2) the sacred-profane theme centering on prayer and the priest, as well as true love and whorehouses; (3) the trio of characters consisting of an American officer, a girl (American, British, Italian), and an Italian officer; (4) the question of marriage; and (5) the ironic theme of "a separate peace."

As for Hemingway's own experiences, and the various ways in which he made use of them in fictions leading to *A Farewell to Arms,* the careful reader discovers in the process the proper answer to the charge that Hemingway's fiction is all "too autobiographical." Hemingway worked out variations on themes; his work was a continuing process. His form of literary art demanded that he take substance from actuality, provide it with mimetic reflection, and produce his own form of combining fiction—but fiction, in these specific instances, not autobiography. Although he himself did not always manage to achieve it, Hemingway once described the desired balance for such fiction: "The more [the writer] learns from experience the more truly he can imagine. If he gets so he can imagine truly enough people will think that the things he relates all really happened and that he is just reporting."[12]

"I had published a novel previously. But I knew nothing about writing a novel when I started it and so wrote too fast and each day to the point of complete exhaustion. So the first draft was very bad. I had to re-write it completely. But in the re-writing I learned much."

—Introduction to the illustrated edition of
A Farewell to Arms, 1948

3

The Two Beginnings
of *A Farewell to Arms*

As primary bounds of enclosure, the beginning and ending of a novel determine to an almost inordinate degree our sense of the form of the novel. And as the most difficult parts of a narrative to write well, they are potential contributors to our sense of difficulty overcome—one of the basic considerations in the appreciation of any art. Studying strategies of opening and closing a novel emphasizes the fact that novels do not pop into life whole, fully clothed and armed, but are born of suffering and travail, and must be nursed and licked into final shape.

One of the reasons *A Farewell to Arms* is critically esteemed is that it is a well-structured novel possessed of a poetically evocative beginning and a dramatically understated conclusion. But Hemingway was beset by considerable difficulties in reaching the beginning and the ending of this novel as eventually published. These difficulties were not new with him: as George Eliot once confided in correspondence, "Beginnings are always troublesome" and "conclusions are the weak point of most authors." Nor was this the first time Hemingway had difficulty with the opening of a novel. The story of how F. Scott Fitzgerald helped him through the initial difficulties of *The Sun Also Rises* is now well known: at various stages of development it began with Jake Barnes, with Niño de Palma; in Hendaye, in Barcelona; but because of Fitzgerald's editorial advice, Hemingway cut deeply into the beginning and wisely started the novel with Robert Cohn, in Paris, thereby ridding the book of much useless stuff.[1] The tale of how Hemingway rewrote the conclusion of *A Farewell to Arms* is also widely known—if less accurately in respect to the manuscript facts (although estimates have varied wildly, there are some forty-one extant attempts at conclusion in the Hemingway Collection).[2]

What is not known is that Hemingway made an even more drastic adjustment in the opening of *A Farewell to Arms* than he did in *The Sun Also Rises,* and with even more radical results. No one has mentioned this radical change before because evidence of it was not known to exist. However, the Hemingway Collection, housed in the John F. Kennedy Library, now includes certain items not listed in Young and Mann's pioneer inventory, *The Hemingway Manuscripts,* and seemingly not available for Baker's *Ernest Hemingway: A Life Story.*[3] Among these items is a two-chapter fragment which is vital to any discussion of the means by which *A Farewell to Arms* was composed and constructed. This remarkable Item 240 is an early—perhaps the original—opening of the novel. It corresponds with a section some eighty pages within the novel as published, corresponding with Chapters XIII and XIV. What these facts indicate is that Hemingway composed the opening and the eleven other essential chapters that constitute Book One of *A Farewell to Arms* as an afterthought— an artistically serendipitous afterthought.

Item 240, unfortunately undated, consists of two chapters done in the author's hand. The first, of eight pages, describes the arrival of the wounded protagonist in Milan, where there is difficulty getting him to an upper floor in an elevator, and where a flustered nurse is unprepared for this first, unexpected American casualty. In substance this manuscript chapter corresponds with Chapter XIII of the published novel, although varying in some detail. The second manuscript chapter, six pages long, describes the protagonist awakening the next morning and being attended by nurses. In substance it corresponds with Chapter XIV of the novel, although varying remarkably in detail of primary importance.

It might be best to summarize and then to explain the facts that indicate Item 240 is either the original or a very early version of the beginning of *A Farewell to Arms:* (1) the first manuscript chapter is unnumbered, but the other is designated "Chapter

Two" in Hemingway's hand; (2) at this stage of development the protagonist is named not Frederic Henry but Emmett Hancock (noteworthy initials when compared with Ernest Hemingway); (3) although "Chapter Two" contains attending nurses, it does not contain anyone resembling Catherine Barkley, or even the name; and it has no reunion scene between the wounded protagonist and his inamorata, as of course Chapter XIV of the novel does; and (4) Item 240 is rougher in prose style and sketchier in detail than Chapters XIII and XIV. Separately each of these facts is indicative; together they represent good evidence that Item 240 is an "ur-opening" of the novel.

It might be supposed that Item 240—consisting in substance of what now stands as the first two chapters of Book Two in the published work—uses the designation of "Chapter Two" because that six-page section so designated was all along meant to be Chapter 2 of Book Two. But that supposition hardly seems likely in the face of another little known fact about the novel—Hemingway did not inject book divisions into *A Farewell to Arms* until *after* it was published serially in *Scribner's Magazine*. These divisions appeared first, as handwritten insertions, in the galleys of the novel.[4]

The second piece of evidence, involving the protagonist's early name, becomes increasingly indicative when placed in context with Hemingway's other manuscripts, galleys, and first forms of publishing, which show that the author often started works of fiction by using the names of actual persons, or names resembling those of actual persons, who were models for characters in those works. *A Farewell to Arms* itself offers an example: not until the novel reached galley stage for serialization did Hemingway finally (with an "E. H." note to the printer) change the name of the actual Count *Greppi* to that of the fictional Count *Greffi*. As noted before, in an early version of "A Very Short Story" he used the name *Ag* (short for Agnes von Kurowsky, upon whom both Ag and Catherine Barkley were modeled) and then for good legal reasons changed it to *Luz*. Also, in a rather notorious instance, he referred to F. Scott Fitzgerald, who was just recovering from his mental crack-up, as "poor Scott" in the first published version of "The Snows of Kilimanjaro," and changed the reference only after Fitzgerald's angry-hurt plea of "would you mind cutting my name?" Thus when the piece came out in *The First Forty-Nine Stories* "poor Scott" gave way to "poor Julian" (who was still ruined by the belief that the rich are not as we).[5] And so also *Emmett Hancock* ("E. H." indeed) of Item 240 gave way to the equally trochaic but less autobiographical *Frederic Henry* in the finished work.

Chapter XIV of *A Farewell to Arms* dramatizes the reunion of Frederic and Catherine Barkley, whose affair, as Rinaldi might put it, "has made progress." Item 240, as previously stated, simply has no Catherine and no reunion of wounded soldier and his girl. The pertinent "Chapter 2" does mention an older, incapable nurse by the name of Miss Walker, who survives in the novel. And it contains an American girl (the first American that Emmett Hancock "had seen for a year"), but she is, alas, doomed to compositional limbo. Described as short, dressed in white, possessed of "dark hair" and "red lips," this countrywoman of Hancock's is an impossible imaginative stretch away from the Scottish Catherine Barkley, who when she finally is born into the world of books is "blonde," "quite tall," with "tawny skin and gray eyes."[6]

Item 240 reflects much the same sketchiness and indecision in respect to prose quality and narrative detail as it does in respect to characterization. Any but the most superficial examination of this portion of the manuscripts (see Appendix A),[7] especially when placed alongside the corresponding sections of the novel as published, will support the conclusion reached here. No reader of Hemingway would describe Item 240 as a polished piece of the author's prose—nor, at the same time, doubt that it stands as the early basis of a somewhat reworked Chapter XIII and a drastically reworked Chapter XIV.

If the author had chosen to continue with the material of Item 240 as the beginning of this novel, *A Farewell to Arms* would obviously have turned into a considerably different work. But it would have been in keeping with a number of Hemingway's narratives which begin *in medias res* with the protagonist already wounded, suffering, incapacitated, or recuperating (including "In Another Country," "The Gambler, The Nun and The Radio," "The Snows of Kilimanjaro," and in a somewhat different vein "A Way You'll Never Be," "Big Two-Hearted River," and *The Sun Also Rises*).[8] In this instance, however, Hemingway would have encountered a problem in narrative strategy much akin to that which confronted Fitzgerald some years later in trying to decide whether to begin *Tender is the Night* with Rosemary Hoyt's story or with that of the Divers (two versions of the novel exist and help prove the difficulty of such opening problems). Hemingway would have had to devise a method to filter in the exposition and introductory narrative material—of prime importance to theme, mode, and character development—which are now contained in the first twelve chapters of *A Farewell to Arms*. In other words, he would have had to eliminate completely, or treat through flashback, the actual wounding of the protagonist; and he would have had to introduce the priest, Rinaldi, and Catherine (or again try cumbersome flashbacks) in Milan during the period of hospitalization and recuperation.

It is almost impossible to say how and when Hemingway reached his final decision on structuring the novel—to begin at the Isonzo front rather than in Milan. Neither biographical data nor manuscript materials provide the answer. The same Fitzgerald who made brilliant editorial recommendations on the opening of *The Sun Also Rises* also made excellent recommendations on this new novel; yet the extant manuscript of his nine pages of notes to Hemingway on *A Farewell to Arms* contains nothing about the opening of the novel—nothing, strangely enough, about anything in the first twelve chapters.[9] And the same Maxwell Perkins who was Hemingway's editor at Scribner's, and did so much to help shape Thomas Wolfe's voluminous outpourings into something resembling novels, was of no discernible help in this instance. In fact, his letters show a wondrous lack of knowledge about what Hemingway was up to during the 1928 compositional period of *A Farewell to Arms*. As late as April 19, 1928, Perkins was still wondering whether Hemingway might have some kind of manuscript "for the fall," and then seems surprisedly overwhelmed by his first and second readings of the novel in typescript on his visit to the author in Key West in 1929.[10] The important thing is that Hemingway, even before reaching what was for him often the second stage of composition —that is, typescript—had done a manuscript version of the opening much as we know it now, beginning with the familiar sentence "In the late summer of that year we lived in a house in a village that looked across the river and the plain to the mountains." At this stage of the composition there are the marks of numerous deletions and insertions, and the materials of Chapter I have not yet been rounded into completion—nor have they been separated from the materials of Chapter II and made into a discrete unit.[11] Nonetheless, Hemingway had by this time made an immense advance in starting and structuring his novel.

II

The first sentence of *A Farewell to Arms* may not be as memorable as "Call me Ishmael" or "It was the best of times, it was the worst of times" or "Happy families are all alike. . . ." The first chapter, however, is one of the most celebrated opening chapters in American fiction, with much of the commentary on it, like that of Edmund Wilson and Ford Madox Ford, concentrating on the pureness of its English prose, the tessellated words standing out as clearly as white stones in a stream. No one seems to have noticed that this two-page chapter of highly cadenced prose has more in common with French literary methods than it does with any other introductory methods in the English or American novel. To find anything like it in intent we must go to Marcel Proust's multivolume *A la recherche du temps perdu*, which begins with a poetic prelude meant to establish the ambience and the imagistic and structural pattern for that entire work. *"L'ou-*

verture," as the introductory is called, is an extended incantation that summons up the past—of flowers, paths, place names, music, people, of madeleine and tea—which unfolds into the fullness of seven volumes.

While this overture of Proust's is sixty pages long, Hemingway's in *A Farewell to Arms* is typical of him in that it is compressed into a mere two pages; but both writers, in proportion to their respective works, were using similar orchestration; and both were relying on a method of composition that had been well known in France from the middle of the nineteenth century on —the *poème en prose.* Beginning with Baudelaire's *Spleen de Paris,* this form spread under the hands of Mallarmé, Rimbaud, Verlaine, Lautréamont, and later writers, notably Max Jacob, St. John Perse, Reverdy, and Gide.[12] Along with free verse, it was part of a reaction against established patterns of rhyme and meter; and although it had no absolutely set pattern of its own, the prose poem achieved coherence through cadenced lines and a unity of tone, mood, and feeling.

Whether Hemingway deliberately, consciously used the prose-poem method in composing Chapter I of *A Farewell to Arms* is impossible to say. We might remember, though, that this was a Hemingway who served much of his literary apprenticeship in Paris, who utilized Proust and Villon in writing "The Snows of Kilimanjaro," and who considered using a title from Flaubert, *The Sentimental Education of Frederick Henry,* for *A Farewell to Arms.*[13] This was the same Hemingway who wrote and spoke French and Spanish with some fluency, who contributed heavily cadenced lines of verse to American and European journals, and who moreover produced something remarkably like prose poems (resembling Max Jacob's "La Guerre" more than the rapt lines of Baudelaire) in those compressed and cadenced paragraphs and sketches that comprise *in our time.*[14]

It remains for someone to do a thorough study of Hemingway's debt to French literary examples and methods, particularly the *poème en prose* approach. Here the concern is mainly with the manner in which he used such a method to form an introduction. Published two years before *A Farewell to Arms,* "In Another Country" employs this technique so admirably that Fitzgerald judged its opening paragraph one of the finest prose pieces he had ever read. As mentioned earlier, that paragraph (which begins "In the fall the war was always there, but we did not go to it any more," and then in a hundred words previews the entire story, imagistically and thermometrically) is the artistic precursor of the opening chapter of *A Farewell to Arms.* [15] Both are English-language approximations of the *poème en prose* method of investing a paragraph, or a series of tightly linked paragraphs, with many of the qualities of modern poetry —such as an insistent cadence, a concatenation of images and potential symbols, and what T. S. Eliot named the objective correlative.[16] These poetic qualities become even more discernible when the opening paragraph is arranged into one of many possible verse presentations:

> In the late summer of that year
> We lived in a house in a village
> That looked across the river and the plain
> To the mountains.
> In the bed of the river there were pebbles
> And boulders, dry and white in the sun,
> And the water was clear and swiftly moving
> And blue in the channels.
> Troops went by the house and down the road
> And the dust they raised
> Powdered the leaves of the trees.
> The trunks of the trees too were dusty
> And the leaves fell early that year
> And we saw the troops marching along the road
> And the dust rising and the leaves,
> Stirred by the breeze,
> Falling
> And the soldiers marching
> And afterwards the road bare and white
> Except for the leaves.

Chapter I of *A Farewell to Arms* consists of five such prose-poem paragraphs arranged in seasonal progression—summer dominating the first two and a half paragraphs, fall the next paragraph and a half, and winter the last paragraph (of two ironically balanced sentences). Its primary images cluster around the weather, the topography, and the historical fact of war. Thus: *sun, dust, leaves* [dropping], *rich crops, green branches* [cut], *rain, mud, permanent rain* and accompanying *cholera; river, plain, mountains, boulders, valley, vineyards; troops, artillery, motor-tractors, ammunition, rifles, cartridges.* It might be said that Hemingway here simply did what scores of World War I novelists did in setting the scene for a war story; but none of the others (not even the poet-novelist Richard Aldington in his powerfully written *Death of a Hero*) approaches Hemingway in the poetic projection of major motifs through an introductory chapter.[17]

From their source here in the opening chapter, these motif-rays shine throughout the novel, providing unity and *claritas.* To a considerable extent, Carlos Baker has shown how this is so in his study of symbolic motifs represented by the initially mentioned mountains and plains, in terms of what happens in the highlands and lowlands throughout the novel.[18] But we could also consider how the introductory "river" leads to the many watery scenes within the novel, in which the protagonist is wounded, in which he cleanses himself of hatred and escapes from the front, and then (by another body of water, Lago Maggiore) escapes to Switzerland, where he and Catherine live in a house where they look out over Lake Geneva. Or we could consider the motif elements of the weatherscape in this remarkable opening—where the green leaves turn dusty and then fall, where the green branches are cut, where the rain leads to cholera and death. Even Catherine Barkley's deadly pregnancy in the rain is prefigured in Chapter I as the troops, "muddy and wet in their capes," moving toward combat, carry cartridge-boxes which "bulged forward under the capes so that the men, passing on the road, marched as though they were six months gone with child."

Structurally, as well as imagistically, this poetic opening of *A*

Farewell to Arms is remarkable in previewing the entire work—particularly in respect to the insistence on temporal and dramatic demarcation. The novel covers approximately two years in the narrative proper, and divides its action into five books which closely approximate the acts of classical tragedy. The first chapter, which might be called "The Masque of the Wet Death," covers about a year and is arranged in three "acts" according to the seasons. Act I, Summer, consists mainly of description and exposition, with comment on troop movement. It merges with Act II, Fall, when the leaves drop and the trees turn black: now the heavy-laden troops move to the combat zone, and the little King and his generals dash back and forth in small gray motor cars. Act III, Winter, is a truncated allegoristic conclusion charged with irony as death arrives in unexpected form: "At the start of the winter came the permanent rain and with the rain came the cholera. But it was checked and in the end only seven thousand died of it in the army." The conclusion of the novel partakes of this same ironic entrance of death in nonmilitary form, as Catherine dies in that civil bastion of security, Switzerland.

Hemingway showed good compositional sense in cutting the first two pages of the novel away from those which now constitute Chapter II and making them into a separate chapter. Actually, those first two pages might have been designated as *"L'ouverture"* or "Prelude" or simply "Introduction," because they do form a chapter unlike any other in the entire novel. This is true not only because of its poetic intensity, its thematic implicativeness, its dramatic unity, but also because of its special narrative viewpoint. Although the remainder of the novel is told from Frederic Henry's first-person-singular point of view, Chapter I is narrated from a first-person-plural point of view—something like the "we" of Faulkner's "A Rose for Emily." This is a special "we" in that it is not all inclusive, or editorial for that matter. It does not signify "we the soldiers," but rather "we the noncombatants, the onlookers not as yet engaged in action," the "we looking across the river and the plain to the mountains," the "we watching troops and King going by," the "we hearing that things are going very badly, and observing what the cholera can accomplish." This same partial "we" reaches over into Chapter II ("we crossed the river in August and lived in a house in Gorizia"), where it modulates to "I" in the first paragraph and finally gives way to Frederic Henry's first-person-singular viewpoint at the beginning of the third paragraph. Here his personal story begins with the scene in which he watches the priest approach in the falling snow.

So the novel begins with a nearly panoramic view which is then changed—in the manner of a camera zooming in for a close-up of Frederic Henry, who then narrates as a singular being. On occasion, however, the novelist-director moves back to that larger view implied by the "we" method of narration. He does this, for example, in the famous speech on patriotic abstractions, where the author shifts from "I" back to "we": "*I* did not say anything. *I* was always embarrassed by the words sacred, glorious, and sacrifice, and the expression in vain. *We* had heard them, sometimes standing in the rain. . . ." But that view is temporary and in the same passage gives way to "you," another large frame of reference, as in "There were many words that *you* could not stand," which in turn brings the view back to *I*, Frederic Henry (p. 191, italics added).

In poetic method, dramatic structure, and narrative overview Chapter I stands out as one of the finest pieces of prefatory composition in all fiction. Here Hemingway displays his considerable skill in employing literary reflectors. Somehow he found ways of making titles, epigraphs, prefatories, interfacing sketches, and envoys (like *"L'envoi"* at the end of *In Our Time*) reflect powerful lights on the main narrative body. Just a year after *A Farewell to Arms* Hemingway exhibited the conscious use of this technique: when he brought out *In Our Time* in its second American edition (1930) he added to it a new piece entitled "An Introduction by the Author," later retitled "On the Quai at Smyrna."[19] As thematic unifier and forecaster, this piece takes its place with the introductory paragraph of "In Another Country" and the epigraph about the frozen leopard appearing in "The Snows of Kilimanjaro" as an example of the reflective method Hemingway used most fully and artistically in Chapter I of *A Farewell to Arms.*

When Maxwell Perkins wrote Hemingway (February 27, 1929) about the title of *A Farewell to Arms,* he said, "I think it is a very good one indeed, though it is one of those titles that is better after you read the book. . . . But even at first sight it is a fine title." These words would apply as well if *Chapter I* were substituted for *title.* This overture of a chapter is good at first sight, but it is "even better after you read the book." In fact, it deserves to be read again, and perhaps again, for among other things it illustrates the genesis of the novel and its unity, showing how its ending was in its beginning, or "beginnings."

"How much re-writing do you do?"

"It depends. I re-wrote the ending of
Farewell to Arms, the last page of it,
thirty-nine times before I was satisfied."

"Was there some technical problem there?
What was it had you stumped?"

"Getting the words right."

—From George Plimpton's interview with
Ernest Hemingway in the *Paris Review,* 1958

4

The Sense of an Ending
in *A Farewell to Arms*

The final act of enclosure in *A Farewell to Arms* consists of less than one page of print, just under two hundred words. In its own way, however, as a dramatic piece of tightly rendered fiction, it proves to be as structurally sound and effective as the evocative "overture" (Chapter I) with which the novel opens.[1] Long admired critically, this conclusion has become one of the most famous segments in American fiction—having been used in college classrooms across the land as a model of compositional compression, and as an object lesson in auctorial sweat, in what Horace called "the labor of the file." The undocumented story of how hard Hemingway worked to perfect the ending of *A Farewell to Arms* approached the level of academic legend. Some tellers of the tale said he wrote the conclusion fifty times, some as high as ninety; others used the safer method of simply saying Hemingway wrote it, rewrote it, and re-rewrote it. Carlos Baker, in his otherwise highly detailed biography, says of the matter only that "Between May 8th and 18th [1929] he rewrote the conclusion several times in the attempt to get it exactly right."[2] In their inventory of the papers available to them at the time, Philip Young and Charles Mann mention only one alternate conclusion separately, and what appears to be either one or two others attached to the galleys for the periodical publication of the novel.[3] One of these is the version Baker published in a collection called *Ernest Hemingway: Critiques of Four Major Novels* under the heading of "The Original Conclusion of *A Farewell to Arms.*"[4] For reasons that will become clear later, this version should be referred to more precisely as "The Original *Scribner's Magazine* Conclusion," for although it was indeed the first to be set in galleys for that publication, it was preceded in composition by at least one other version in handwritten form, and probably more.[5]

As the papers now indicate, Hemingway deserved to be taken pretty much at his word when he told George Plimpton he had written the conclusion thirty-nine times. Depending upon a number of small variables, and upon what one is willing to call an attempt at conclusion, there are between thirty-two and forty-one elements of conclusion in the Hemingway Collection of the John F. Kennedy Library.[6] These appear in typescript and in handwritten form, and run from one or two sentences to as many as three pages in length. Some of the short elements show up again in the fuller attempts, helping to produce combination endings that consist of fragments arranged in varying alignments. There is, of course, no guarantee that Hemingway did not write even more variations: some could have been lost, destroyed, forgotten. But those that exist in the Hemingway Collection represent a rich fund of critical information capable of revealing the process of rejection-selection that the author went through to reach "the sense of an ending."[7] Not only can we see in this scattered process the thematic impulses which run through the novel and which the author was tempted to tie off in many of these concluding attempts; but we find in it the figurative seven-eighths of Hemingway's famous "iceberg" that floats beneath the surface of the art object. In one sense, most of the concluding attempts that are to be examined here may be considered as artistically subsumed under what finally became *the* ending of *A Farewell to Arms.* Understanding them should lead to a better understanding of it, and the novel as a whole.

All of the conclusions in the Hemingway Collection presuppose Catherine's death. Hemingway chose to present the actual death in understated, summary fashion at the very end of the penultimate section of the last chapter: "It seems she had one hemorrhage after another . . . and it did not take her very long to die."[8] Presumably, that summarization did not take much writing effort. In itself Catherine's death, although beautifully prepared for in the first three quarters of the last chapter, is not one of Hemingway's moments of artistic truth—like the flat cinematic projection of Maera's death in *In Our Time*, or the elaborate mythic flight of Harry in "The Snows of Kilimanjaro." It contains none of the asyntactical eloquence of Frederic's near-death, when he feels his soul slip out of his body like a handkerchief from a pocket and then return to corporeal life (p. 57). This is, after all, Frederic Henry's story, and it is his reaction to Catherine's death that had to be depicted with revelatory force. All of the variant conclusions that Hemingway wrote for the novel are attempts to epitomize Henry's traumatized perception—from which, years later, the story unfolds.

Most of the variant attempts fall into natural clusters that can be referred to as: (1) The *Nada* Ending, (2) The Fitzgerald Ending, (3) The Religious Ending, (4) The Live-Baby Ending, (5) The Morning-After Ending, (6) The Funeral Ending, (7) The Original *Scribner's Magazine* Ending, and (8) *The* Ending. But a final grouping of (9) Miscellaneous Endings is needed initially to accommodate five brief attempts that have little in common with each other or any of those in the previously mentioned categories.

These five are all single-page holographs, four mere fragments (see Appendix B, 9). Two echo material in Chapter I by mixing rain with the thought of many men and women dying in wartime; and they conclude that knowing about the death of many is no consolation to someone mourning the death of a specific person. Another reaches back to Henry's nearly fatal wounding, as he compares the traumatic effect of Catherine's death on him with that produced by the physical wound: in both instances the numbness wears off and only pain remains. Still another of these miscellaneous attempts makes use of the old saying "See Naples and die," concluding bitterly that Naples is a hateful place, a part of that unlucky peninsula which is Italy. The last, and most interesting, of these attempts briefly entertains the notion of suicide: the narrator realizes he can end his life just as arbitrarily as he writes finis to his narrative; but he decides not to and later is not "sorry" about his decision. Through the first four of these attempts, and a number of others later, we can observe Hemingway trying to find the right linear motif with which to tie off the novel—climatological, psychological, or geographical. With the introduction of suicide in the fifth, however, we are reminded that the end of any novel, not just this, is in a sense a prefigurement of the novelist's death. All of the attempts to conclude a novel mirror the life choices of the creator; and the conclusion of a life can be as arbitrary and/or artistically appropriate as the conclusion of a novel.

"The *Nada* Ending" is represented by three fragmentary attempts to express Henry's sense of being-and-nothingness after Catherine's death (see Appendix B, 1). His mind is stunned and produces only a negative response, a form of *nada*. He senses that everything is gone—all their love—and will never be again. But at the bottom of one of these handwritten fragments an added note declares, with some of the ambiguity found at the end of "A Clean, Well-Lighted Place," that "nothing" is lost. The bluntest of the three attempts simply states that there is nothing left to the story, and that all the narrator can promise is that we all die.[9] This nihilistic attitude echoes Henry's earlier statement made to a hungry animal nosing around a garbage can: "There isn't anything, dog." And it is this same negative tonality, expressed dramatically, which dominates the ending Hemingway eventually devised for the novel.

Although related to the *nada* group, "The Fitzgerald Ending" deserves separate discussion because of the peculiar editorial circumstances surrounding it. As is now well known, F. Scott Fitzgerald helped Hemingway considerably in choosing the proper opening of *The Sun Also Rises*. What has not been well known is that he also advised Hemingway editorially on a number of matters in *A Farewell to Arms:* Item 77 in the Hemingway Collection consists of nine handwritten pages of Fitzgerald's comments on the typescript of the novel.[10] He so admired one passage in the book that he noted it in the typescript as being "one of the most beautiful pages in all English literature"; and later, in his last note on the novel to Hemingway, he wrote: "Why not end the book with that wonderful paragraph on p. 241 [pp. 258–259 in print]. It is the most eloquent in the book and would end it rather gently and well." The passage referred to is that in which Henry, in Chapter XXXIV, contemplates how the world "kills the very good and the very gentle and the very brave," and concludes "If you are none of these you can be sure it will kill you too but there will be no special hurry." Hemingway did try to use the passage as an ending, once by itself in holograph (see Appendix B, 2) and once with other elements in polished typescript (Appendix B, 7). As we know, he rejected both possibilities and kept the passage intact within the novel. In a letter to Hemingway (dated June 1, 1934), defending his own *Tender Is the Night*, Fitzgerald shed much light on his own sense of an ending, as well as Hemingway's and Joseph Conrad's:

> The theory back of it I got from Conrad's preface to *The Nigger*, that the purpose of a work of fiction is to appeal to the lingering after-effects in the reader's mind. . . . The second contribution . . . was your trying to work out some such theory in your troubles with the very end of *A Farewell to Arms*. I remember that your first draft—or at least the first one I saw—gave a sort of old-fashioned Alger book summary . . . and you may remember my suggestion to take a burst of eloquence from anywhere in the book that you could find it and tag off with that; you were against this idea because you felt that the true line of a work of fiction was to take a reader up to a high emotional pitch but then let him down or ease him off. You gave no aesthetic reason for this—nevertheless, you convinced me.[11]

"The Religious Ending" (Appendix B, 3) represents one of Hemingway's least negative variants and perhaps the most potentially incongruous. Had any form of this conclusion been retained, *A Farewell to Arms* would have emerged with a much different emphasis in theme—one depending heavily upon a passage (in Chapter III) that has puzzled many readers. This is the place where Henry tries to express the evanescent wisdom of the priest: "He had always known what I did not know and what, when I learned it, I was always able to forget. But I did not know that then, although I learned it later" (p. 14). What is the *it* which Henry learns, and when does he learn it? The usual interpretation stresses *it* as love: the priest's love of God, Frederic's love for Catherine; and the connection between agape and eros. But Hemingway's experiments with religious conclusions for the novel reveal the *it* of the priest as transcending any mundane love, which can be snuffed out by death. Under these circumstances, the *it* that Henry learns "later" is that everything will be all right if, as these fragments indicate, "you believe in God and love God." No one, the narrator concludes, can take God away from the priest, and thus the priest is happy. With such a conclusion the priest would have emerged as the supreme mentor of this *Bildungsroman,* not Rinaldi, Count Greffi, or even Catherine. However, a question imbedded in two of these religious attempts helps to explain why this kind of conclusion was rejected. Henry wonders how much of what the priest has is simply luck, how much is wisdom—and how do you achieve what the priest has if you are not "born that way"? It is, eventually, a question of deterministic grace.

Another fairly positive ending that Hemingway dropped is one in which Frederic and Catherine's child lives, instead of dying as it does in the novel. Two of these "Live-Baby Endings" (Appendix B, 4) were written to be inserted into the penultimate section of the last chapter, to precede Catherine's death. But the third makes it clear that Hemingway attempted to provide an ending in which the fact of birth, of new life, mitigates death. In this version Henry finds it difficult to talk about the boy without feeling bitter toward him, but concludes philosophically that "there is no end except death and birth is the only beginning." Stoic as these words may sound, they nevertheless tend to mitigate the deeper gloom produced in the novel by the death of both mother and child. In several senses "The Live-Baby Ending" would have meant another story; and with a touch of editorial wisdom reflecting that of the author, Henry realizes "It is not fair to start a new story at the end of an old one. . . ."

The concluding element Hemingway worked on longest and hardest was one built on a delayed reaction, "The Morning-After Ending" (see Appendix B, 5 and 7). In holograph and typescript form, ten variations on this conclusion exist as more or less discrete elements; five are incorporated into combination conclusions, including "The Original *Scribner's Magazine* Ending," as published by Baker, and both the "original" and "first-revised" conclusions, as represented in Michael Reynolds' *Hemingway's First War*.[12] In all of these Frederic returns, after Catherine's death, to the hotel where they had been staying: after some time he falls asleep because he is so tired; waking to a spring morning, he sees the sun shining in through the window and for a moment is unaware of what has happened. The moment of realizing Catherine is gone—something of a dull, truncated epiphany—is rendered in two ways. In most versions, including those published by Baker and Reynolds, Henry merely experiences a delayed response—"then suddenly to realize what had happened." But in other versions his recognition of his predicament is stimulated by a burning light bulb: seeing it still lit in the daylight brings double illumination. Through this simple device, Hemingway placed Frederic Henry among those other protagonists of his who, like children, have trouble with the dark—including the Old Man in "A Clean, Well-Lighted Place," the Lieutenant in "Now I Lay Me," and Nick Adams in "A Way You'll Never Be," who confesses, "I can't sleep without a light of some sort. That's all I have now." His words could stand for Frederic Henry in these versions of the conclusion. He too, earlier in the novel, gives utterance to nocturnal blues: "I know that the night is not the same as the day: that all things are different . . . the night can be a dreadful time for lonely people once their loneliness has started. But with Catherine there was almost no difference in the night except that it was an even better time" (p. 258). Without Catherine, all that is left is a light bulb burning in the night, announcing on the morning after that she is dead.

In one instance Hemingway employed "The Morning-After Ending" as a transitional device to achieve "The Funeral Ending" (Appendix B, 6). The initial material of this one-page holograph is essentially the same as that described in the Baker version, but this variant does not end with the flat statement of "that is the end of my story." Instead, Hemingway here makes one of his first attempts to conclude with an obverse-iteration method: Henry says that he could tell about his meeting with the undertaker and "the business of burial in a foreign country," but, the implication is, as the sentence trails off, he will not. The same kind of obverse iteration is incorporated into the two other attempts at this funeral conclusion: people die and they have to be buried, but the narrator does not have to tell about the burying, or the resulting sorrow. Henry tells us—somewhat reversing the earlier notion of suicide—that in writing "you have a certain choice that you do not have in life."

It is impossible to state with certainty what the exact order of composition was for all the variant elements of conclusion, since they are undated.[13] But there are good indications that the combining form of "The Original *Scribner's Magazine* Ending" (Appendix B, 7) was the penultimate version. For one thing, most of the variations in this group (five of eight) are highly polished typescripts. For another, these versions combine many of the previously mentioned attempts as contributing elements—including the "morning-after" idea, as well as the funeral, suicide, lonely nights, the Fitzgerald suggestion, and the obverse-iteration method of stating-but-not-stating what happened after that particular night in "March nineteen hundred and eighteen." Most significantly, one version of this combining conclusion very nearly became the ultimate one—to the extent of having been set in galleys for the serial publication of the novel.

Hemingway scribbled a note to hold matters on this conclusion, however, and then eventually supplanted it with the dramatic version that we now have. If he had not done so, *A Farewell to Arms* would have ended in the old-fashioned manner of tying up the loose narrative ends in summary fashion. For in the original galley version Frederic Henry says that he could, if he wanted to, tell his reader many things that had happened since that night when Catherine died. He could tell how Rinaldi was cured of syphilis (answering the question of whether Rinaldi did indeed have the disease); how the priest functioned in Italy under Mussolini (indicating that this is a story being told years after its occurrence); how Simmons became an opera singer; how the loudly heroic Ettore became a Fascist; and how the loyal Piani became a taxi driver in New York. A variant of this conclusion places Piani in Chicago instead of New York and hints that something unpleasant happened to the socialist-deserter Bonello in his home town of Imola. In all of the variants of this combining ending, however, Henry decides he will not tell about all of these people, or about himself, since that time in 1918, because all of that would be another story. This story ends with Catherine's death, or more specifically with the dawn of his awakening to that fact on the morning after.

Hemingway reached this point in his search for an ending by August 1928. He made some galley adjustments on this combination ending early in June 1929. But he still was not satisfied; the last phase of his search began, and on June 24, 1929, almost ten months after completion of the first full draft of the novel, Hemingway reached "*The* Ending" (see Appendix B, 8).[14] Tracing through all of the elements of conclusion for *A Farewell to Arms* in the Hemingway Collection is like accompanying the captain of a vessel who has been searching through uncharted waters for a singularly appropriate harbor: then suddenly after all this pragmatic probing there appears the proper terminus to his voyage, and yours, something realized out of a myriad number of possibilities. In less figurative terms, "*The* Ending" emerges suddenly as the product of what Mark Schorer has aptly called "Technique as Discovery."

Even in the very last phase of this process Hemingway continued to write and rewrite to discover what should be said on the final page of the novel as a result of what had been said in the preceding three hundred and forty pages. Including the ultimate choice, there are extant five holographic variants of "*The* Ending." They are closely related, and they remind us that Hemingway once said the most difficult thing about writing was "getting the words right." With cross-outs, replacements, realignments, these final five efforts demonstrate technique as discovery in the most basic sense of getting the words right, which leads to getting the right message, the right form.

All five are basically alike in form and substance. They are all examples of the dramatic method of showing, rendering, rather than telling. They all contain the descriptive element of the rain, the dramatic action of clearing the hospital room and taking leave of Catherine's corpse, and the narrative reflection that none of it is any good. All include the most important sentence in the actual conclusion: "It was like saying good-by to a statue." But they all state these matters in slightly different ways, using different positions for various phrases and ideas, achieving different emphases and effects. For example, Hemingway moved the sentence about "saying good-by to a statue" around like a piece in a puzzle: in one instance he tried for maximum effect by restating it as the very last sentence of the novel (see Appendix B), but evidently thought that too obvious and placed it eventually in its penultimate position, where it is now followed by the line that runs "After awhile I went out and left the hospital and walked back to the hotel in the rain."

Kenneth Burke reads that last sentence as a small masterpiece of understatement and meteorological symbolism: "No weeping here," he declares; "Rather stark 'understatement.' Or look again, and do you not find the very heavens are weeping in his behalf?" Burke finds here an echo of Verlaine's line "It rains in my heart as it rains on the town."[15] This critical hunch receives support from the most interesting variant of *"The* Ending," which takes from the heavens a touch of religious consolation. In this version, out of Frederic Henry's reflections, comes a brief line obviously modeled on the Beatitudes: "Blessed are the dead that the rain falls on. . . ." It has poetic lilt and fits in beautifully with the weather imagery throughout the novel; and at first the reader is inclined to think Hemingway made the wrong decision in dropping it from the final ending. But further consideration reveals a sense of craft wisdom. Having previously rejected "The Religious Ending" that features the happiness of the priest, and having depicted the inefficacy of Henry's prayers for the dying Catherine, the author here remained artistically consistent. In eliminating even this nub of religious consolation, he obtained the flat, nihilistic, numbing conclusion that the novel now has.[16]

Here again, in this last instance of rejection as in all of the preceding instances, we are reminded that Hemingway's best fiction is the product not only of *what has been put in* but also of *what has been left out.* "Big Two-Hearted River" is perhaps the most obvious example of this propensity in Hemingway's work; it took critics years to fill in the deliberate gaps in that story, by borrowing information from other pieces of Hemingway's fiction, in order to get a full reading of what they sensed was a powerful work of suppressed drama. Hemingway intuitively understood that sublimated words form part of any message as uttered, providing as they do a psychological tension and an emotional context for that utterance. He spoke of trying to achieve "a fourth and even a fifth dimension" in his fiction, and formulated a synecdochic theory for the-thing-left-out: "I always try to write on the principle of the iceberg. There is seven-eighths of it underwater for every part that shows. *Anything you know you can eliminate and it only strengthens your iceberg.* It is the part that doesn't show."[17] Examining some forty attempts at conclusion for *A Farewell to Arms* provides a rare inside view of that theory: it reveals what the author knew, the submerged, suppressed part of the message. Moreover, it opens to critical view an auctorial process of exclusion-inclusion, an exercise of willed choice, that closely parallels the life-choices of the protagonist-narrator. Thus we can see that the published conclusion is possessed of an extraordinary tension and literary power because it sublimates, suppresses, and/or rejects the same things that Frederic Henry does —including religious consolation; hope for the future and the continuance of life (as reflected in "The Live-Baby Ending" and in the summary of characters in the combination endings); the eloquence of courage and beauty (expressed in "The Fitzgerald Ending"); and even the negative solution of suicide (suggested in one of the miscellaneous endings). In this instance, everything that the author and the protagonist knew and eliminated went into strengthening this tip of the iceberg.

Conceived as it was in the spirit of rejection, the conclusion of *A Farewell to Arms* is in and of itself a compressed exemplification of the process of rejection and negation. The only thing that Hemingway retained from all the preceding attempts at ending the novel is the core of "The *Nada* Ending." He eventually wrote finis to the story by bringing its materials down to a fine point of "nothingness," and thus left the reader with the same message Frederic Henry gives the hungry dog in the last chapter: "There isn't anything, dog." Within the short space of the one hundred and ninety-seven words that comprise the conclusion, Hemingway uses *nothing* three times and a series of some thirteen forms of negation, in various phrases like "No. There is nothing to do," "No. . . . There's nothing to say," and simply "No, thank you." In the process, Frederic Henry rejects the attending physician's explanation of the Caesarean operation, his offer of aid, and the nurse's demand that he stay out of Catherine's room. But the most powerful form of rejection occurs in the final paragraph of the book, when Henry says his last farewell to arms: "But after I got them [the nurses] out and shut the door and turned off the light it wasn't any good. It was like saying good-by to a statue." He rejects the corpse; it rejects him. Even in this ultimate scene of nullification Hemingway uses his principle of omission in a subtle manner: he says nothing about Frederic's embracing or kissing the statue-like corpse, although it is a rare reader who does not interpolate some such act. Also, Hemingway does nothing here to remind the reader that with Catherine Lieutenant Henry had come to accept the night, the darkness, and found that with her it was an "even better time" than the day. But now Henry deliberately turns off the light, as though to test his alliance with Catherine, and finds that the warmth and companionship of love are inoperative, defunct. We can thus understand why, in many of the combination endings, Henry is described as sleeping with the light bulb turned on in the hotel room. Night will never be "a better time" for him again.

II

To estimate the worth of the conclusion Hemingway finally composed for *A Farewell to Arms,* and to get beneath its surface meaning, we should consider some of the literary and philosophical propensities involved in the conclusions of novels in general. E. M. Forster, in his sensible and perceptive *Aspects of the Novel,* makes what may be the most commonly repeated statement on the subject: "If it was not for death and marriage I do not know how the average novelist would conclude."[18] Indeed, Forster believes that endings constitute "the inherent defect of novels," partly because authors simply tire and then force their characters to do and say things to bring about a specious conclusion, or because they behave like Henry James in forcing characters to fit a predetermined plot and conclusion. Forster proves to be an early advocate of what has recently been referred to as "open-end" forms of fiction: he recommends that novelists look not to the drama for complete-seeming endings, but to music and its trailing reverberations as a concluding analogue. "Expansion," he declares: "That is the idea the novelist must cling to. Not completion. Not rounding off but opening out."[19]

Forster was in partial agreement with the nineteenth-century English novelist George Eliot. In correspondence, she confided that "beginnings are always troublesome," but "conclusions are the weak point of most authors." She added, however, that in her estimation, "some of the fault lies in the very nature of a conclusion, *which is at best a negation.* "[20] Frank Kermode, who quotes Eliot's remarks in *The Sense of an Ending,* takes exception to them by declaring: "Ends are ends only when they are not negative but frankly transfigure the events in which they are immanent."[21]

This is an important, carefully worded statement, and *The Sense of an Ending* is an important contribution to the small critical circle of literary eschatology. Limited by thesis, it is an informative and illuminating treatise on literary conclusions as derived from apocalyptic bases. With considerable scholarly and rhetorical force, Kermode traces a line of descent from public apocalypse to private crisis in literary endings, and demonstrates that some of our best modern poetry, drama, and fiction partake of this eschatological endgame. The line of descent runs roughly from St. John of Patmos through the Shakespeare who wrote *King Lear* to the Blake who wrote the visions, to a host of twentieth-century writers like Yeats, T. S. Eliot, Beckett, Camus, Sartre, and Robbe-Grillet. What these writers have in common, according to Kermode, is a system of literary conclusions that stand as transfiguring revelations. These are Kermode's true endings, which "transfigure the events in which they were immanent." This definition demands a final convolution, the sense of a world ending with either a bang or a whimper, a universal metamorphosis. Although it certainly fits works which are basically apocalyptic, in Kermode's expanded sense, this definition of an ending as something which exists *only* when transfiguration takes place seems if not wilful at least overly stringent.

How do the conclusions of many excellent and well-known novels meet Kermode's concept of a true ending? He points to *Anna Karenina* as a novel with a proper sense of ending, by which he means the epiphanated conversion of Levin to some transcendent concept of man's ability to will goodness. But there are really two "endings" to Tolstoy's novel, just as there are two intercrossing plots; and to discuss Levin's inner transformation without considering Anna Karenina's suicidal *negation* is to miss half the point of the novel, which is based on antithesis rather than simple peripety. *War and Peace,* which Forster selects for its musical aftereffect, ends with no transfiguration in sight; it ends, in fact, with a somewhat dull essay on historical and theological necessity (part of the essayistic material in the novel which Hemingway advised readers to skip).

A brief review of the endings of some famous novels, chosen almost at random (closest to hand on a worthy bookshelf), may throw some light on the problem of concluding and upon the specific accomplishment of Hemingway in *A Farewell to Arms*. *Tom Jones* ends in marriage and an old-style summary of what happens to "the other persons who have made any considerable figure in this history." *Vanity Fair* ends with a welter of events, death and marriage, a summary of the characters, and a final word from the stage-managing narrator: "Come, children, let us shut up the box and the puppets, for our play is played out." *Madame Bovary* ends with funeral considerations in respect to Emma, followed by Charles' death, the disposition of the child, and the ironic triumph of viciousness, as represented in the last sentence of the book, which simply says of M. Homais, "He has just received the cross of honor." After the death of Bazarov, *Fathers and Sons* ends with a summary of characters and a visit to the graveyard, and also with a considerable amount of sentimental consolation: "the flowers . . . tell us, too, of eternal reconciliation and of life without end." *Crime and Punishment* ends with the forced repentance of Raskolnikov in the arms of a reformed prostitute and under the wings of Russian Orthodoxy. Along with the long anticlimactic section of *Huckleberry Finn,* Dostoevsky's must be one of the most suspect and controversial endings in all of literature. (Hemingway, incidentally, showed critical concern about the conclusion of Twain's book, advising readers to stop reading at the place where Huck makes his decision to help Nigger Jim escape slavery.)

These great novels of the eighteenth and nineteenth centuries are certainly not the works of what Forster calls "the average novelist," but they do support his observation about the dependence upon death and marriage in reaching conclusions. Except in one instance, however, they contain none of the transfiguration which Kermode insists upon for a true ending. His apocalyptic description becomes more meaningful in such twentieth-century novels as Kafka's *The Trial* and Camus' *The Stranger.* Fitzgerald's conclusion of *The Great Gatsby,* with its green light effulgence and pervasive sense of continental ruination, also tends toward the apocalyptic. And in *The Sound and the Fury, The Bear,* and especially *Light in August,* Faulkner approaches transfiguration through the disruption of chronological time and blasts of discordant activity.

But not all modern novels utilize such concluding means. The long interior ramble of Molly Bloom which ends *Ulysses* is difficult to define as transfiguring—except in the sense that all great literary figures transcend the bounds of ordinary beings. There have to be other considerations of what constitutes the proper, the right, the true ending for a work of literature. To begin with, conclusions cannot be made or judged by some outside measure; it is self-evident that they must fit the beginnings and middles of the works which they terminate. Concordance and decorum are as important considerations as claritas. It would be nonsensical, for example, to expect the conclusion of Steinbeck's *The Grapes of Wrath* (not to mention one of Dickens' or C. P. Snow's works) to end in some great contortion of events leading to transfiguration. Even though *The Grapes of Wrath* contains some of the materials for social apocalypse, its conclusion is true to the naturalistic body of the book, and to its sociological sentiment, as Rose of Sharon quite literally provides a starving man with her own milk of human kindness.

Although, then, Kermode provides us with some excellent insights into the literary endgames of works that are essentially tragic in nature, cataclysmic in event, there are other legitimate ends besides these. *The Sense of an Ending* is an admittedly restrictive analysis; and what is needed to balance out Kermode's definition of an ending is some understanding of Martin Heidegger's "zero" (the quintessential "not" or "naught") and of Henry James' geometrical figure, the "circle" of artistic appearance. At the very least, they help account for the conclusion which a twenty-nine-year-old American intuited, through the exercise of his craft, for *A Farewell to Arms.*

It is doubtful that Hemingway read Heidegger's *Existence and Being.* Much more important than any possible influence is the parallel working of minds—the one philosophical, the other artistic—in seeking out answers to the question of nothingness. In *Existence and Being,* Heidegger argues the supremacy of philosophy over natural science, because philosophers can ask the prime metaphysical question that includes "Nothing," or "non-being," while scientists are stuck with the question of "what-is." How, Heidegger asks, can we account for *something* issuing forth from *nothing?* And how are we to relate what-is to nothing? Science simply ducks the question. Classical metaphysicians dealt poorly with the same question, conceiving of "nothing," in Heidegger's words, as "unformed matter which is powerless to form itself into 'being' and cannot therefore present an appearance." Their dictum on the subject was *"ex nihilo nihil fit"*—nothing comes from nothing. But Christian theologists changed that concept by placing God outside the circle of nothingness and having Him create the entire universe from it.

Heidegger believes that we are projected to our fullest moments of truth, toward an understanding of "nothing" and its relation to being, by boredom (which brings us to the abyss of existence), by "the presence of the being—not merely the person —of someone we love," and by a dread that comes to us when "what-is" slips away and we are faced with "nothing." Thus "Dread reveals Nothing." This is what Heidegger means by *"Dasein,"* which he defines in part as "being projected into nothing." It is interesting to compare Heidegger's language in the search for "nothing" and the words of the middle-aged waiter in Hemingway's "A Clean, Well-Lighted Place." Heidegger writes:

> Where shall we see Nothing? Where shall we find Nothing? In order to find something must we not know beforehand that it is there? Indeed we must! First and foremost we can only look if we have presupposed the presence of a thing to be looked for. But here the thing we are looking for is Nothing. Is there after all a seeking without pre-supposition, a seeking complemented by a pure finding?[22]

Hemingway writes:

What did he fear? It was not fear or dread. It was nothing that he knew too well. It was all nothing and a man was nothing too. It was only that and light was all it needed and a certain cleanness and order. Some lived in it and never felt it but he knew it all was nada y pues nada y nada y pues nada. Our nada who art in nada nada be thy name thy kingdom nada thy will be nada in nada as it is in nada. . . . Hail nothing full of nothing, nothing is with thee. He smiled and stood before a bar with a shining steam pressure coffee machine.

"What's yours?" asked the barman.

"Nada."

"Otro loco más," said the barman and turned away.

Had this particular barman been reading Heidegger he would most certainly have uttered the same words he uses on Hemingway's middle-aged waiter—"Another crazy one." The barman, however, has not been undergoing an experience in "Da-sein," has not been projected into nothingness.

Hemingway, like Heidegger, only in fictive terms, is dealing with the metaphysical question of all times; and the middle-aged waiter recapitulates much of Christian dogma, except that he places God within, rather than outside, the circle of nothingness: "Our nada who art *in* nada. . . ." This parodistic statement may or may not be atheistical, but it is heretical. The principal function of an atheistical universe is to *make itself* out of nothing (cosmologists have not yet solved the problem of how this was done). The principal function of Christian theology is to separate the idea of God from the idea of nothing and illustrate how that deity created the universe out of nothing. The principal function of a literary artist is to imagine and make felt the "nothing" which Heidegger seeks, and then out of that nothing create the something which is his art. The middle-aged waiter in "A Clean, Well-Lighted Place" speaks more for artists than he does for waiters when he speaks of the it-ness of being: "It was a nothing that he knew too well. . . . It was only that and light was all it needed and a certain cleanness and order." "Light," indeed. "And God said, 'Let there be light'; and there was light." All that the literary artist needs to add to that is the idea that in the beginning was the word, and the word is with the writer, whose job it is to "get the words right," with a "certain cleanness and order."

A Farewell to Arms ends with no apocalyptic bang or whimper, only words that dwindle away to nothing. Lieutenant Henry is left at the end with much the same nothing sensed by the middle-aged waiter in "A Clean, Well-Lighted Place," by Santiago in *The Old Man and the Sea,* and by the protagonists depicted by Hemingway in a book of short stories entitled, appropriately enough, *Winner Take Nothing.* Henry takes the nothing with which *A Farewell to Arms* ends and out of it performs the artist's task of making his tale, whose conclusion rings with his own words of advice: "There isn't anything, dog." If a cosmic boom-bust cycle is suggested here, so is the ploy of an intricate modernist writer like John Barth, who introduces his *Lost in the Funhouse* with the makings of a Möbius strip whose twisted continuous message reads "ONCE UPON A TIME THERE WAS A STORY THAT BEGAN ONCE UPON A TIME THERE WAS A STORY THAT BEGAN ONCE. . . ." Hemingway's novel dwindles to the nothingness of Catherine's death and then springs to full life out of the disruptive force of that nothingness and then again dwindles to the point of nothing. . . . The mutual inclusiveness of this kind of cycle parallels Heidegger, who declares: "The old proposition *ex nihilo nihil fit* will then acquire a different meaning, and one appropriate to the problem of Being itself, so as to run: *ex nihilo omne ens qua ens fit*: every being, so far as it is a being, is made out of nothing. Only in the Nothingness of *Da-sein* can what-is-in-totality . . . come to itself."[23]

The true conclusion of *A Farewell to Arms,* the one Hemingway sweated to conceive and perfect, consists of the fourth segment of the last chapter. This short segment is characterized by extraordinary dramatic compression, by a succinct recapitualization of leading motifs, by implicative understatement, by a high percentage of negating phrases, and by the final effect of dwindling away to nothing, with a seeming rupture of chronological time. (It should be said that the first three segments of the last chapter pay full attention to chronological and biological time, using Frederic Henry's three dull meals and Catherine's labor pains as metronomic devices.)

The action of this conclusion makes it as much a playlet as "Today Is Friday." The action begins with the surgeon's explanatory regrets and his offer, which is rejected, to take Henry to his hotel. The second part consists of Henry's forcible entrance into the room containing Catherine's body and his ejection of both nurses: " 'You get out,' I said. 'The other one too.' " In the third section he shuts the door, deliberately turns out the light, and makes his unsatisfactory, inexplicit farewell to arms. The final element of action, a kind of one-sentence coda, marks his exit from the hospital and his lonely walk in the rain toward the hotel. To manage all of this activity (in one hundred and ninety-seven words) without seeming to hurry it and mar the presentation, to compress the events in a manner consonant with the inherent emotional tension—these are considerable artistic achievements.

The supreme touch in the conclusion, however, is the provision of a single encapsulating image in the line "It was like saying good-by to a statue." This is an independent creation, based on nothing, which attempts to metaphorize beyond the bounds of knowing, to enclose being and nothingness. As mentioned before, Hemingway shifted that line around in the variants he wrote, trying to find its proper position, and finally deciding on penultimate placement. Out of the very last sentence of the novel— "After a while I went out and left the hospital and walked back to the hotel in the rain"—Kenneth Burke fashions a renewal reading, in which the rain signifies sorrow and rebirth. "Add to that," Burke says, "the fact that the hero is there returning in the rain to his hotel. Does not such a destination stand for the potentiality of new intimacies?"[24] Although that reading may have merit on its own, it receives no support from the variant conclusions Hemingway wrote.[25]

The image of the statue is more deserving of close attention than the rain in this instance. The truth about death and marriage (and E. M. Forster seems to find little difference between them) as subjects of novelistic conclusion is that, in a sense, all novels end in death. When the book is closed, all of the characters "die," no matter their fictive status. The magical advantage literature has over human life is that we can open the book again and all the characters will pop back into full-blown life. The truth is that all novelists create to murder, and in some instances murder to create. Hemingway reduces Catherine Barkley to the level of a cold piece of stone, but an artistically shaped stone. The Pygmalion myth is here acted out in reverse, and then put right again. For out of that "statue" of the penultimate sentence of *A Farewell to Arms* springs the entire warm and loving story that constitutes the novel, a story told years after its occurrence. Out of the dread nothingness of Catherine's death, which takes Frederic Henry and the reader to the edge of the abyss, is fashioned "what-is-in-totality" the novel.

The art wisdom implicit in the conclusion of *A Farewell to Arms* is critically revealed in Henry James' statement of the central problem of ending novels, which he made in the preface to *Roderick Hudson:* "He [the writer] is in the perpetual predicament that the continuity of things is the whole matter for him, of comedy and tragedy; that this continuity is never broken, and that, to do anything at all, he has at once intensely to consult and intensely ignore it." As the variant endings here examined indicate, Hemingway struggled mightily with the problem of breaking and yet not breaking continuity in his narrative design. His solution to the problem in *A Farewell to Arms* amounts to a latter-day exemplification of James' astute directive on literary conclusions: "Really, universally, relations stop nowhere, and the exquisite problem of the artist is eternally but to draw, by a geometry of his own, the circle within which they shall happily *appear* to do so."[26]

Appendix A

The Original Beginning

Item 240 in the Hemingway Collection of the John F. Kennedy Library consists of two handwritten chapters (eight and six pages long, respectively) that constitute the earliest beginning of *A Farewell to Arms* known to exist. The first chapter is unnumbered and unidentified; the second is marked "Chapter Two." These are reproduced here by permission of Mary Hemingway and the Kennedy Library. Brackets and parentheses are used in the text to indicate authorial deletions.

The train came into the station at Milan early in the morning.

The ambulance stopped and they lifted out the stretcher. The jolt at the moment of [lifting] moving made a [sickening pain] feeling; [it was a feeling like] as of dropping in an elevator except that [here] it was pain.

"Go easy," said the Lieutenant. "Take it softly, softly."

They carried the stretcher into the hospital and set it down. From the door of the ambulance to the door of the hospital the Lieutenant [passed] was in the street. It was early morning and they were watering the street and [the] he saw the market place and an open wine shop. Then it was hospital. The stretcher would not go in the door of the elevator. There was an elevator man and a smell of hospital. They could carry him upstairs on the stretcher or they could lift him off the stretcher and carry him up in the elevator. He listened to them discussing it. They decided to take him up in the elevator. At the moment of lifting him off the stretcher there was the pain and he waited, knowing it never went past a certain point. That was his theory but the pain kept on and passed that point and he was suddenly sick cold inside and in back of his ears, far inside between the bones.

"Son of a bitch," he said and the [two] man who was carrying the upper half of him smiled and said it would be over in a minute. The Lieutenant saw the doors of the elevator closed and the grill shut and the 4th floor button pushed by the porter. The porter had a grey mustache and looked worried.

The elevator rose slowly on a column of water. The Lieutenant [saw] looked into the face of the man whose arms were around his shoulders.

"Heavy?" he asked.

"Feather weight," said the man. "You know what that means?"

"Sure," said the Lieutenant. [and] The elevator rose [past the iron balconies] steadily and then stopped. The man at the feet opened the door. They stepped out with him. There were several doors. Holding him they rang a bell. No one came. Then the porter came up the stairs.

"Where are they?" the stretcher bearers asked.

"I don't know," said the porter.

"Get somebody."

The porter rang the bell. He knocked on the door. Then he opened the door and disappeared. He came back and with him was an elderly woman wearing glasses. Her hair was [disarranged untidy] only partly done; and she wore a nurse's dress.

"I can't understand," she said. "I can't understand Italian."

"I can speak English," the Lieutenant said. "They want to put me somewhere."

"None of the rooms are ready. There's no patient expected." She tucked at her hair.

"Show them any room where they can put me," the Lieutenant said.

"I don't know," she said. "There's no patient expected. I couldn't put you in just any room."

"Any room will do," said the Lieutenant. Then to the elevator porter in Italian. "Find an empty room."

"They are all empty," said the porter. "You are the first patient."

"For the love of Christ," the Lieutenant said slowly, "take me to some room." He was trying not to cry. The pain had passed the point at which he had made himself believe it always would stop and was going back and forth from the flesh into the bone. The porter went in the door, followed by the gray haired woman and came running back. "Follow me," he said. The men moved, carrying the Lieutenant, down a hall way to an open door and into a room with drawn blinds.

"I can't put on sheets," the woman said. "The sheets are locked up."

The Lieutenant did not speak to her. "There is money in my pocket," he said to the porter. "In the buttoned down pocket." The porter took out the money. The two stretcher bearers stood beside the bed, their caps in their hands. "Please give them five lira apiece and five lira for yourself," the Lieutenant said. "My papers are in the other pocket. You may give them to the nurse."

The stretcher bearers [saluted and went out] thanked him. "Good bye," the Lieutenant said. "And many thanks." They saluted and went out.

"Those papers," the Lieutenant said, "describe my case and the treatment already given."

The [old] elderly woman looked at them. There were three [of them] papers and they were folded. "I don't know what to do," she said. "I can't read Italian [and the]. I can't do anything without the doctor's orders. She commenced to cry and put the papers in her apron pocket. "Are you an American?" [There were tears] she asked crying.

"Yes," said the Lieutenant. "Please put the papers on the table by the bed."

It was dim and cool in the room. The pain was [very light] thin [as spider web] now. The porter stood by the bed. He had a nice face and he was very kind. The wops were nice. "You can go," the Lieutenant said to him. "You can go too," he said to the nurse. "What is your name?"

"Mrs. Walker."

"You can go Mrs. Walker. I think I can go to sleep. I have not been to sleep for five days." He smiled. "No that's my bowells. I haven't moved my bowells for five days. No seven days. I haven't been to sleep for five months."

He was alone in the room. It was cool and did not smell like a hospital. There was a big armoire with a mirror. He could not see himself in the mirror. He knew he had a beard and he would have liked to see it. It was the first beard he had ever grown. He rubbed his cheek very softly against the pillow, barely moving it. Moving his head started the pain again and he lay still feeling it lessen. He was happy on the smooth firm bed and he lay without moving, hardly breathing, enjoying the lessening pain and the coming of sleep.

CHAPTER TWO

[When he (a) woke there was sunlight in the room and a girl was (standing by the bed) moving around the room.]

When he awoke there was sunlight in the room and a girl was moving around. He lay [and] still and watched her. She was short, dressed in white, her hair was dark and she had red lips. She saw he was awake and came over to the bed. She was the first American girl he had seen for a year. He smiled at her. She was very pretty.

"We haven't been able to get the Doctor," she said. "He's gone to Lake Como. We didn't know a patient was coming. What's wrong with you anyway?"

"I'm wounded," the Lieutenant said. "In the feet, legs, and hands and my head's been caved in."

"What's your name?"

"Hancock, Emmett Hancock."

"What is your rank?"

"[Tenente] Lieutenant."

"What are you doing in the Italian Army? How did they happen to send you here?"

"I don't know. They heard there was an American hospital and [they asked me] they thought I'd like to go there."

"Put this in your mouth." She put a thermometer under his tongue. ["Don't talk]

"In the Italian hospital," Hancock said, "they put it under your armpit."

"Don't talk," the nurse said. She put her hand on his forehead. He looked at her appealingly. The pain had jumped [into action] instantly. She patted his forehead. The pain went up and down like a fever chart.

"Don't do that," he said. "[I can't stand to have my head touched.] Please don't touch my head."

She took out the thermometer, shook it and read it. "How is it?" he asked.

"[Your tem] The temperature is normal," she said. "Would you like the bed pan?"

"All right," he said. He could not move and she helped him. He was [very] embarrassed but enjoyed it.

"I'm afraid it isn't any use," he said. "I don't have control of that muscle."

She undressed him and another nurse came and they gave him a bath. They put clean sheets on the bed without moving him. He enjoyed it all except the pain. The second nurse was young too and Irish. No woman except his mother, the nurse they had had when they were children, and his sisters when they were all little had ever seen him naked before. He was embarrassed but it was [exciting] pleasant. They wanted to wash his head too but he would not let them.

"But there are big pieces of dirt right into the scalp," the nurse called Miss Fairbanks said. "It's absolutely full of dirt."

"You can't wash it yet," he said. "Let it alone a while."

They put a clean pyjama jacket on him and left him under the clean sheet. When they were gone and he was alone in the bright sunny room suddenly that muscle over which he had no control relaxed. He called but no one came. He lay quiet under the sheet and let it happen. He felt better but ashamed. A new nurse came in to see him and he told her he had made a mess. She said he was a poor boy and it did not matter. Another nurse came and they changed the sheet [and], cleaned him off and washed him clean with soap and warm water. They left him alone again. He felt better and then there was a sharp griping pain and it had happened again. They had fixed a bell for him to call with beside the bed. They came and were as nice about it as they had been the first time but they gave him a rubber sheet.

"I'm awfully embarrassed," he said. "I wish I could help it."

It happened twice more that day and it did a great deal to make him feel less like an officer [and a gentleman]. He had liked the nurses and hoped to make a good impression and instead all he did was ruin bed sheets and have to be looked after like a baby. This was a fine hospital. All the nurses were nice. It was bright but cool. There was a balcony outside the window and [at noon] the bed was high enough so he could see out past the stone railing of the balcony and [see] look over the tile roofs of [the town] Milan. At noon they brought in a fine meal but he was not hungry.

"Can I have wine?" he [said] asked.

"Not unless the doctor says so."

"They gave it to me in the hospital at the front."

"If the doctor says you can have it you can have it."

"When is the doctor going to come?"

"As soon as he comes back from Lake Como."

"Isn't there another doctor?"

"No. He's the only one. We didn't expect any patients yet."

[He had not wanted to leave the hospital at the front. He had not wanted to come back to Milan except for the nurses. He had wanted to have the nurses and have them make a fuss over him. He wanted one to fall in love with. But these had not attracted him, instead they]

When he shut his eyes he could see the hospital at the front. He could see it with his eyes open. There was no mosquito netting for the beds and your orderly sat beside the cot with a brush made of newspaper cut into strips and whisked the flies away. Two men picked you up and carried you into the dressing room every time they dressed your wounds. That gave them a chance to fix the bed. At night no one could sleep and you all sang. When your orderly went to sleep in the daytime [the] and stopped brushing way the flies they settled on your face if you were asleep and left things in the corners of your eyes and in your nose. The doctor swabbed them out with a cotton on a stick. The doctor said that since the dead had been buried and the Piave cleaned up after the offensive the flies would lay eggs anywhere.

[The only editorial change made in these two chapters as presented here is the regularization of contractions; Hemingway sometimes put the apostrophe in, and sometimes did not. His spelling of *bowels* (as *bowells*) has been kept in the text, as well as his use of the singular *lira* in Italian for the plural *lire.*]

Appendix B

Concluding Variants

The descriptive materials in this appendix, as well as the examples that follow, are also presented with the permission of Mary Hemingway. These materials are contained in the Hemingway Collection of the John F. Kennedy Library, specifically in the following Items: 64, 65, 66, 70, and 73. These are the actual designations used in the Collection.

The author of this study is responsible for the categorization of the materials presented, and for any errors that may have occurred. The categories under which these elements of conclusion have been arranged are in a few instances tentative and overlapping. A definitive textual study of the manuscript elements of *A Farewell to Arms* remains to be done, with full collation and notation. Here each draft, even each fragment, of an attempt at a conclusion for the novel has been treated as a variant. Each is designated by "V" in the schema which follows.

The *Nada* Ending (1)

V–1: Handwritten paragraph of approximately 25 words, beginning "That is all. . . ." (All it promises is that we die.)

V–2: Handwritten fragment of approximately 50 words, also beginning "That is all. . . ." (Contains ironic reference to God's eye on the sparrow.)

V–3: Handwritten fragment of approximately 20 words, beginning "And then I knew. . . ." (Declares that nothing will be the same again.)

V–4: Handwritten sentence fragments on one page of approximately 35 words, the first beginning "In the end. . . ." (Last element declares that nothing is gone.)

The Fitzgerald Ending (2)

V–5: Handwritten paragraph of approximately 100 words. "Everyone who lived through the war had"—crossed out. Begins

"You learn a few things. . . ." (Contains sentiment about the good and the beautiful to be found on pp. 258–259 of the novel. For *Fitzgerald Ending* used in combination with other elements see section 7 of this Appendix.)

The Religious Ending (3)

V–6: Handwritten page (marked 323) of approximately 150 words, beginning "It is a mistake. . . ." (Speaks of the wisdom of the priest and asks whether it is wisdom or luck, a form of grace.)

V–7: Handwritten page (marked 324) of approximately 150 words, beginning "Also you will bore them" which is crossed out; beginning again "At first the nights," which is also crossed out; and beginning again "You learn the wisdom of the priest. . . ." (Repeats the message of the priest's love of God and asks whether it is luck.)

V–8: Handwritten page with two short variants, first variant "religious," approximately 25 words, beginning "The thing is. . . ." (Says everything will be all right if you believe in God.)

The Live-Baby Ending (4)

V–9: Handwritten page of approximately 125 words, beginning "There are a great many more details," a passage which is crossed out; begins again with "I could tell about the boy. . . ." (States that the child represents a new start and it would be unfair to make a new start.)

V–10: Handwritten page (marked 638) of approximately 100 words, beginning "What's the matter with the baby. . . ?" (Admits the baby is not important, only Catherine.)

V–11: Handwritten page (marked insert page 641) of approximately 100 words, beginning "After a little while. . . ." (Consists of dialogue assurance by physician that baby is a "fine boy" and alive.)

The Morning-After Ending (5)

V–12: Handwritten paragraph of approximately 80 words, beginning "I walked that night. . . ." (Summarizes action from hospital to sleep in hotel room and awakening to spring morning with realization of death.)

V–13: Handwritten page of approximately 110 words, beginning "That is all," "I walked home," "It was raining," "They said" —all crossed out; beginning "It was raining outside. . . ." (Rewords essentially the same material as V–12, though with varying phrases.)

V–14: Handwritten page of approximately 135 words, beginning "It was raining outside the hospital. . . ." (Essentially the same as V–12 and V–13, though with additional detail including mention of "elevator," "porter," etc.)

V–15: Typed paragraph of approximately 75 words, beginning "When I woke the sun was coming in. . . ." (Introduces the idea of the electric light still on, alerting the protagonist to what had actually happened.)

V–16: Typed paragraph of approximately 65 words, beginning "When I woke the sun was coming in. . . ." (Almost a duplication of V–15, this variant changes phrasing slightly.)

V–17: Typed fragment of approximately 45 words, beginning "then as I woke completely. . . ." (Much like V–15 and V–16, this variant introduces idea of a "physically hollow" feeling.)

V–18: Typed paragraph with handwritten concluding element added of approximately 185 words, beginning "It was raining outside. . . ." (This includes all elements of "elevator," "porter," "sun," "spring morning," and signaling electric light.)

V–19: Typed paragraph (marked E322) of approximately 170 words, beginning "I walked in the rain that night. . . ." (Contains all elements of V–18 but varies slightly in wording and designates, with handwritten insertion, "that night in March nineteen hundred and eighteen.")

V–20: Typed paragraph (marked 322) of approximately 185 words, beginning "It was raining outside," which is crossed out;

beginning "I walked in the rain. . . ." (Varies only slightly from V–18 and V–19, and includes indication "The End" in brackets.

The Funeral Ending (6)

V–21: Handwritten fragment of approximately 30 words, beginning "When people die. . . ." (States that burials and undertakers do not have to be written about.)

V–22: Handwritten paragraph of approximately 90 words, beginning "After people die. . . ." (Declares that writing offers choices in omission that life does not.)

V–23: Handwritten paragraph of approximately 100 words, beginning "After people die. . . ." (Much like V–22, this variant adds the idea that "numbness" after someone's death changes to "sorrow," which then "blunts.")

The Original *Scribner's Magazine* Ending, or The Combination Ending (7)

V–24: Handwritten page (marked 322) and possible fragment addition (marked 323) of approximately 240 words, beginning "I walked," which is crossed out; beginning "They said there was nothing," which is crossed out; beginning again "All sorts of things," which is crossed out; and then beginning "It is a long time. . . ." (This combines the "morning-after" element with the funeral.)

V–25: Original three-page (marked 650–652) handwritten version of the ending which in revised form was printed in galleys for *Scribner's,* approximately 450 words, beginning "There are a great many more details. . . ." Contains the word "End" approximately halfway through page (probably 651) but then continues with a coda beginning "Many things have happened. . . ." (This combines funeral element with summarization of what became of characters afterward. Coda enters tragic interruption of life.)

V–26: Three-page handwritten revision of V–25 (marked 650

bis–652), approximately 330 words, beginning "There are a great many more details. . . ." (This combines the funeral, morning-after, and summarization of character elements; a smoother, less wordy version of V–25.)

V–27: Typed page of approximately 290 words (marked 322), beginning "There are a great many more details. . . ." (This combines summary of characters and morning-after.)

V–28: Typed page of approximately 240 words, beginning "There are a great many more details. . . ." (Simply slightly shorter version of V–27, with addition of electric light stimulus.)

V–29: Typed page of two paragraphs, approximately 240 words, beginning "There are a great many more details . . . ," and including in parentheses the words "The End." (Major difference from V–28 is presentation of material in two paragraphs rather than one.)

V–30: Typed page of three paragraphs, approximately 270 words. This is the typescript base for what Baker published as "The Original Conclusion" in *Ernest Hemingway: Critiques of Four Major Novels;* and for what Michael Reynolds published as "First Revised Ending" in *Hemingway's First War.* Begins "There are a great many more details. . . ." and has appended to it in handwritten form the words "The End." (Except for minor changes in phrasing essentially the same as V–28 and V–29.)

V–31: Two pages of typescript (marked 322–323) consisting of three paragraphs, approximately 460 words, beginning "It is a long time since March nineteen hundred and eighteen. . . ." (This is the fullest of the combination endings. It includes everything in the original *Scribner's Magazine* conclusion and tacks on the material suggested by F. Scott Fitzgerald. See section two of this Appendix, V–5.)

The Ending (8)

V–32: Handwritten page of approximately 130 words, beginning "They went out and I shut the door. . . ." (This includes the

Beatitude line "Blessed are the dead that the rain falls on," and centers the "statue" line.)

V–33: Two handwritten pages of approximately 130 words, beginning " 'I know there's nothing to say. . . .' " (In this variant a nurse speaks of "rules"; the "statue" line is repeated and placed at the very end.)

V–34: Handwritten page of approximately 120 words, beginning "But after I had gotten them out. . . ." (This variant crosses out "statue" line in middle and places it for the first time in the penultimate position.)

V–35: Handwritten paragraph of approximately 110 words, beginning "But after I had gotten them out. . . ." (This is the next to last variant in the entire process. It differs from the final version mainly in cross-outs and the inclusion of the idea that "there would still be something"—that is, in Henry's being alone with Catherine's corpse.)

V–36: This is *the* ending: handwritten page of approximately 105 words, beginning "He went down the hall. . . ." (This segment attaches to the previous element—see V–33—which includes discussion with the physician. This last portion varies from the published conclusion only in spelling *got* as *gotten.* Otherwise they are identical.)

Miscellaneous Endings (9)

V–37: Handwritten paragraph of approximately 65 words, beginning "That was in March nineteen hundred and eighteen. . . ." (Says that there were "many other dead for the rain to fall on.")

V–38: Handwritten paragraph of approximately 50 words, beginning "That was in March. . . ." (Adds women to the "plenty" of men that were killed that month.)

V–39: Handwritten page of approximately 100 words, beginning "I was too numb to realize it," which is crossed out; and then beginning "It was like a wound that you do not feel at first. . . ." (Discusses delayed shock and the blame for Catherine's death.)

V–40: Handwritten fragment of approximately 40 words, beginning "Maybe you have never been alone. . . ." (Contains saying "See Naples and die.")

V–41: Handwritten fragment of approximately 50 words, beginning "Your life does not stop," which is crossed out; and then beginning "You can stop your life. . . ." (Entertains possibility of suicide.)

Example Endings

[Brackets are used in the examples to indicate authorial deletions.]

EXAMPLE: "The *Nada* Ending" (1)

That is all there is to the story. Catherine died and you will die and I will die and that is all I can promise you.

EXAMPLE: "The Fitzgerald Ending" (2)

[Everyone who (went) lived through the war had]

You learn a few things as you go along and one of them is that the world breaks everyone and afterward many are strong at the broken places. [But those that will] Those it does not break it kills. It kills the very good and the very gentle and the very brave impartially. If you are none of these you can be sure it will kill you too but there will be no special hurry.

EXAMPLE: "The Religious Ending" (3)

You learn a few things as you go along and one of them is never to go back to places. It is a good thing too not to try [and] too much to remember very fine things [too much] because if you do you wear them out and you lose them. A valuable thing too is never to let anyone know how [how] fine you thought anyone else ever was because they know better and no one was ever that splendid. You see the wisdom of the priest at [our] the mess who has always loved God and so is happy. And no one can take God away from him. But how much is wisdom and how much is luck to be [built] born that way? And what if you are not built that way?

EXAMPLE: "The Live-Baby Ending" (4)

I could tell about the boy. He did not seem of any importance then except as trouble and God knows that I was bitter about him. Anyway he does not belong in this story. He starts a new one [story]. It is not fair to start a new story at the end of an old one but that is the way it happens. There is no end except death and birth is the only beginning.

EXAMPLE: "The Morning-After Ending" (5)

I walked in the rain that night in March nineteen hundred and eighteen from the hospital to the hotel where Catherine and I had lived and went in the gate and up the driveway and in through the revolving door. I spoke to the porter; he gave me the key and I rode up in the elevator, stepped out, shut the door, walked down the hall and unlocked the door and went into the room where we had lived and there undressed and got into bed. Finally I slept; I must have slept because in the morning I woke. When I woke the sun was coming in the open window and I smelled the spring morning after the rain and saw the sun on the trees in the courtyard and in [the] that moment of waking everything was the way it had been [and there was nothing gone]; then I saw the electric light still on in the daylight by the head of the bed and [then] I knew what it was that had happened and [that] it was all gone now and that it would not be that way any more.

EXAMPLE: "The Funeral Ending" (6)

After people die you have to bury them but you do not have to write about it. You do not have to write about an undertaker

nor the business of burial in a foreign country. Nor do you have
to write about that day and the next night nor the day after nor
the night after nor all the days after and all the nights after while
numbness [becomes] turns to sorrow and sorrow blunts with use.
In writing you have a certain choice that you do not have in life.

EXAMPLE: The Original Basis for "The *Scribner's Magazine*
Ending" (7)

There are a great many more details, starting with [the] my first
meeting with an undertaker and all the business of burial in a
foreign country and continuing on with the rest of my life—
which has gone on and [will probably] seems likely to go on for
a long time. I could tell how Rinaldi [recovered from] was cured
of the syphylis and lived to [learn] find that the technique acquired in wartime surgery is [rarely employed] not of much practi-
cal use in peace. I could tell how the priest in our mess lived to
be a priest in Italy under Fascism. I could tell how Ettore became
a Fascist and the part he took in [Fascism] that organization. I
could tell [what] the kind of singer whatsis name became. [I could
tell how I made a fool of myself by going back to Italy.] I could
tell about how Piani [became] got to be a taxi driver in [xxxxx]
New York. But they are all parts of [an old story] something that
was finished. I [suppose it was finished at the Tagliamento] do not
know exactly where but certainly finished. Piani was the least
finished but he went to another country. Italy is a country that
[a man] every man should love once. I loved it once and lived
through it. You ought to love it once. There is less loss of dignity
in loving it young or, I suppose, living in it [or at least live in it,]
is something like the [utility] need for the classics. I could tell
what I have done since March nineteen hundred and eighteen
[and] when I walked that night in the rain [alone, and always from
then on alone, through the streets of Lausanne] back to the hotel
where Catherine and I had lived and went upstairs to our room
and undressed and got into bed and slept, finally, because I was
so tired—to wake in the morning with the sun shining; [and] then

suddenly to realize what [had happened] it was that had happened. I could tell what has happened since then. [The world goes on but only seems to stand still for certain people] but that is the end of the story.

End

[Lots of] Many things have happened. Things happen all the time. [xxxxxxx] Everything blunts and the world keeps on. You get most of your life back like goods recovered from a fire. It all keeps on as long as your life keeps on and then it keeps on. It never stops. It only stops for you. [A lot] Some of it stops while you are still alive. [A lot] The rest goes on and you go on with it. [You can stop a story anytime. Where you stop it is the end of that] On the other hand you have to stop a story. You stop it at the end of whatever it was you were writing about.

EXAMPLE: Variant of *"The* Ending" (8)

They went out and I shut the door and turned off the light. The window was open and I [could] heard it raining in the courtyard. [It wasn't any good. She was gone. What was there was not her.] After a while I said goodbye and went away. It was like saying goodbye to a statue. But I did not want to go. I looked out the window. It was still raining hard. Blessed are the dead that the rain falls on, I thought. Why was that? I went back. Good-bye, I said. I have to go I think. It wasn't any good. I knew it wasn't any good. I thought if I could get them all out and we could be alone we would still be together. But it wasn't [not like that] any good. It was like saying goodbye to a statue.

EXAMPLE: Miscellaneous Endings (9)

You can [not] stop your life the way you stop a story [except by] but you do not do it and afterwards you are not sorry. It stops for a while by its-self and then it goes on again.

Notes

Introduction

1. Both Carlos Baker and Michael Reynolds use Hemingway's correspondence with Maxwell Perkins in stating that the novel began as a short story: see Baker's *Ernest Hemingway: A Life Story* (New York: Scribner's, 1969), p. 190; and Reynolds' *Hemingway's First War: The Making of "A Farewell to Arms"* (Princeton: Princeton University Press, 1976), p. 20. However, the earliest material dealing with the novel in the Hemingway Collection at the John F. Kennedy Library appears to be Item 240, which consists of fourteen holograph pages constituting two chapters numbered pp. 1–8 and 1–6, respectively. See Chapter 3 of this study for a full discussion of this material.

2. The information in this and the following paragraph is based on Baker, pp. 187–199.

3. See Cleanth Brooks, R. W. B. Lewis, and Robert Penn Warren, *American Literature: The Makers and the Making* (New York: St. Martin's Press, 1973), II, 2259.

4. See particularly pp. 74–76 and 107, 113.

5. Both this and the preceding quotation from Hemingway come from Item 75 in the Hemingway Collection, which includes both holograph and typescript materials.

6. Perkins correspondence in the Hemingway Collection: Western Union telegram, February 13, 1929. Perkins had discussed the possibility of serializing the novel with Hemingway in a letter dated August 8, 1928, in which he says that Scribner's had previously paid Edith Wharton and John Galsworthy about $10,000 for long serials.

7. *Scribner's Magazine*, May 1929, p. 493.

8. This publication data is from Audre Hanneman's *Ernest Hemingway: A Comprehensive Bibliography* (Princeton: Princeton University Press, 1967), pp. 23–24.

9. Robert Herrick, "What Is Dirt?" *The Bookman*, November 1929, pp. 258–262.

10. Henry Seidel Canby, "Story of the Brave," *Saturday Review of Literature*, October 12, 1929, pp. 231–232.

11. Reynolds, p. 7.

12. Hemingway Collection, Item 77; see the last page of these notes.

Chapter 1

1. Kenneth Burke, "Literature as Equipment for Living," in *Visions and Revisions in Modern American Literary Criticism*, ed. Bernard Oldsey and Arthur O. Lewis (New York: Dutton, 1962), pp. 194 ff.

2. After diplomatically granting a section of Czechoslovakia to Germany in 1938, British Prime Minister Neville Chamberlain boasted somewhat prematurely that he had achieved "peace in our time." He proved to be a more orthodox reader of the Book of Common Prayer than Hemingway but a much less accurate prognosticator. Chamberlain was succeeded by Winston Churchill just before Dunkirk.

3. *In Our Time* concludes with "The Big Two-Hearted River," which depicts an ironic kind of traumatized and insecure peace.

4. Such titles would include in the first category *Green Hills of Africa*, "Up in Michigan," "On the Quai at Smyrna," "Out of Season," "Cross-Country Snow," "An Alpine Idyll," "After the Storm," "The Sea Change," "Homage to Switzerland," "Wine of Wyoming." And in the second category: *A Moveable Feast*, "God Rest you Merry, Gentlemen," "A Natural History of the Dead," *Torrents of Spring*. (Actually "The Sea Change" and *Torrents of Spring* overlap categories—the first having literary reference to Shakespeare's *The Tempest;* and the second, coming directly from Turgenev, has obvious climatological application.)

5. Hemingway Collection, Item 64.

6. "The Art of Fiction XXI," an interview of Ernest Hemingway by George Plimpton, *Paris Review* 18 (Spring 1958), 83.

7. Michael Reynolds, *Hemingway's First War: The Making of* A Farewell to Arms (Princeton: Princeton University Press, 1976), p. 295.

8. Philip Young and Charles W. Mann, *The Hemingway Manuscripts: An Inventory* (University Park: Pennsylvania State University Press, 1969), p. 18. (Hemingway did, incidentally, use "Along With Youth" as a title for one of his poems.)

9. Reynolds, pp. 50–53.

10. Carlos Baker, *Ernest Hemingway: A Life Story* (New York: Scribner's, 1969), p. 199.

11. Except for these last three titles, which are attached to various manuscripts, all of the other titles mentioned in these lists (thirty of them) are from Item 76 of the Hemingway Collection, a two-page list written in pencil. Cf. Reynolds, pp. 295–297.

12. Reynolds, p. 295.

13. *The Oxford Book of English Verse: 1250–1900*, ed. Arthur Quiller-Couch (Oxford: Oxford University Press, 1912). All references throughout this chapter in respect to this work are to the 1912 edition; this and other editions were available to Hemingway by 1928.

14. Ibid., p. 53.

15. Ibid., pp. 142–143.

16. Reynolds, p. 64.

17. T. S. Eliot, *Collected Poems: 1909–62* (New York: Harcourt, Brace, 1963), pp. 8–12.

18. Baker, p. 190.

19. Reynolds, p. 295.

20. Baker, p. 199. (Hemingway is rather obviously echoing Samuel Pepys' often ribald diary and its refrain of "And so to bed.")

21. *The Life and Minor Works of George Peele*, ed. David H. Horne (New Haven: Yale University Press, 1952), p. 170.

22. *The Oxford Book of English Verse*, pp. 142–143.

23. Baker, p. 199.

24. For fuller discussion of this point, see Chapter 4 of this study.

25. Ernest Hemingway, *A Farewell to Arms*, Modern Standard Authors Edition (New York: Scribner's, 1953), p. 191. Except where specific manuscript reference is made, all subsequent references to the novel are to this standard and readily available edition of *A Farewell to Arms*.

26. In 1927, two years before *A Farewell to Arms*, Hemingway published fourteen stories under the title of *Men Without Women*. These and other stories alerted critics to Hemingway's psychological, and marital, trait of withdrawing from women. Edmund Wilson has written about many of these stories as exemplifying battle-of-the-sexes themes. Philip Young has viewed much of Hemingway's work, particularly the Nick Adams stories, as continuations of the withdrawal process from Hemingway's threatening mother. Bernard Oldsey states, in a discussion

of "The Snows of Kilimanjaro," "Thus Harry's imaginary flight constitutes the ultimate in a long line of withdrawals from female arms; part
of its motivating power comes from the immemorial fear of castration."
("The Snows of Ernest Hemingway," as reprinted in *Ernest Hemingway*, ed. Arthur Waldhorn [New York: McGraw-Hill, 1973], p. 71.)

27. As reprinted in Arthur Waldhorn's *A Reader's Guide to Ernest
Hemingway* (New York: Farrar, Straus, 1972), p. 81.

28. In translation: "But where are the snows of yesteryear?" and
Hemingway's answer: "In the piss hole with all such stuff."

29. *The Oxford Book of English Verse*, p. 53. Hemingway placed
great emphasis on this collection, as indicated.

30. *A Farewell to Arms*, p. 204. Charles Anderson makes good use
of this passage in an article entitled "Hemingway's Other Style," *Modern Language Notes* 76 (May 1961), 434–442.

Chapter 2

1. Robert Scholes, *Structuralism in Literature* (New Haven: Yale
University Press, 1974), p. 132.

2. Wilfrid Sheed, "Desperate Character," a review article in *The New
York Review of Books*, May 12, 1977, pp. 31–34.

3. *Islands in the Stream* is a fusion of three separate manuscripts as
arranged by Mary Hemingway and Charles Scribner, Jr. See Audre
Hanneman, *Supplement to Ernest Hemingway: A Comprehensive Bibliography* (Princeton: Princeton University Press, 1975), p. 25.

4. *Hemingway and The Sun Set* (Washington, D.C.: NCR, Microcard Editions, 1972).

5. We could also add to this list such estimable works as Simone de
Beauvoir's *The Mandarins* and most of Thomas Wolfe's work, including
Look Homeward, Angel.

6. *A Moveable Feast* (New York: Scribner's, 1964), Preface.

7. *Studies in Classic American Literature*, Compass Books edition,
(New York: Viking, 1964), p. 2.

8. W. K. Wimsatt, Jr., and Monroe C. Beardsley, "The Intentional
Fallacy" and "The Affective Fallacy," in *The Verbal Icon*, 2d Noonday
edition (New York: Noonday Press, 1960), p. 3.

9. Michael Reynolds, *Hemingway's First War: The Making of "A
Farewell to Arms"* (Princeton: Princeton University Press, 1976), pp.

181–219. Reynolds devotes about a quarter of his study to the problem of character sources, including an entire chapter to the "Search for Catherine."

10. Reynolds devotes another quarter of his study to the research Hemingway did for his depiction of the war in Italy and particularly for the Caporetto retreat; see Reynolds, pp. 87–160.

11. For a revisionist account of Italy's performance in World War I, see A. J. Whyte, *The Evolution of Modern Italy* (New York: Norton, 1965). Whyte sees the Caporetto affair as part of a larger series of events and depicts Italy's recovery and strong actions afterward in a favorable light.

12. *By-Line: Ernest Hemingway* (New York: Scribner's, 1967), p. 215.

Chapter 3

1. See Philip Young and Charles W. Mann, "Fitzgerald's *Sun Also Rises:* Notes and Comment," *Fitzgerald/Hemingway Annual 1970* (Washington, D.C.: NCR Microcard Editions, 1970), pp. 1–9; and Carlos Baker, *Ernest Hemingway: A Life Story* (Princeton: Princeton University Press, 1969), pp. 149–155.

2. Depending upon variables too numerous to mention here, and upon what one is eventually willing to call a "conclusion," there are between thirty-five and forty-one extant forms of conclusion in the Hemingway Collection in the John F. Kennedy Library.

3. The Curator of the Hemingway Collection has keyed corresponding items there to the listings in Young and Mann's *The Hemingway Manuscripts: An Inventory* (University Park: Pennsylvania State University Press, 1969); but nothing in Young and Mann, or in Baker's biography, corresponds to Item 240 in the Hemingway Collection, which consists of fourteen pages in holograph, numbered pp. 1–8 and 1–6. Michael Reynolds' book *Hemingway's First War* (Princeton: Princeton University Press, 1977) deals specifically with the compositional order of *A Farewell to Arms.* But for some reason or other, although Reynolds appears to have had full access to the Hemingway Collection, he makes no mention whatsoever of the fourteen manuscript pages that constitute Item 240. See Reynolds, particularly pp. 20–51.

4. Hemingway Collection, Items 64 through 74, which include the collected manuscripts, typescripts, and galleys of *A Farewell to Arms.*

See also the serial installments of the novel, without book designations, as published in the May through October issues of *Scribner's Magazine,* 1929.

5. Baker, 290–291.

6. Ernest Hemingway, *A Farewell to Arms,* Modern Standard Authors edition (New York: Scribner's, 1953), p. 18.

7. See Appendix A; a close parallel reading of the two typescript chapters along with Chapters XIII and XIV of the novel shows how expertly Hemingway reworked these materials.

8. When the author of this study mentioned this early opening of *A Farewell to Arms* in conversation with Robert Penn Warren, he was taken with Warren's supportive reply of "Why, sure, that's exactly what he *would* do."

9. Item 77 of the Hemingway Collection consists of nine pages of F. Scott Fitzgerald's holographic comments on the novel—probably Item 65, the typescript original of the setting copy of *A Farewell to Arms.* These nine pages may simply be a portion of his comments, since his first suggestion deals with Chapter XIV; the probability is that earlier comments have been lost. As mentioned previously, Fitzgerald's final comment on the typescript is: "A beautiful book it is." Hemingway's somewhat embarrassed rejoinder (initialed "E. H.") is: "Kiss my ass."

10. Hemingway Collection: uncatalogued letters from Maxwell Perkins to Ernest Hemingway, dated April 19, 1928, and January 25, 1929.

11. Reference here is to Item 64 in the Hemingway Collection. Although undated, this pencil holograph evidently predates Item 65 (a typescript version of the novel) and Item 66 (a carbon copy used to set print). In Item 64 Hemingway provided no division between the materials constituting Chapters I and II as published; these materials were all part of "Chapter 1" in the holograph.

12. C. A. Hackett writes clearly and well of the methods and ideas of such *poème en prose* writers in his *Anthology of Modern French Poetry* (Oxford: Blackwell & Mott, 1952).

13. Item 76 of the Hemingway Collection is a two-page (one-sheet) list of possible titles. As the list indicates, Hemingway actually fashioned four possible titles from Flaubert, all centering on the idea of "education" (as noted on pp. 18–19, 24–25 of this study).

14. *in our time* probably owes more to the *poème en prose* method

than any other Hemingway work. See Hackett, p. 105, for "La Guerre."

15. Bernard Oldsey, "The Snows of Ernest Hemingway," in *Ernest Hemingway: A Collection of Criticism*, ed. Arthur Waldhorn (New York: McGraw-Hill, 1973), pp. 67–68.

16. See Linda W. Wagner's chapter on "Hemingway as Imagist" in her *Hemingway and Faulkner: Inventors/Masters* (Metuchen, N.J.: Scarecrow Press, 1975). Although Wagner does not discuss the *poème en prose* or French influences, she very clearly traces certain of Hemingway's poetic tendencies in prose. See also Michael Reynolds, p. 56: independently, he and the author of the present study were enough impressed by the poetic quality of Hemingway's opening lines to present them in verse form.

17. Aldington's *Death of a Hero* is more of a war novel as such than any of Hemingway's novels and Aldington's imagistic treatment of the frozen horror of winter warfare is very powerful, but *A Farewell to Arms* is a fuller and more accomplished piece of literary art.

18. Carlos Baker, *Hemingway: The Writer as Artist* (Princeton: Princeton University Press, 1952); specifically, the chapter entitled "The Mountain and the Plain."

19. Audre Hanneman, *Ernest Hemingway: A Comprehensive Bibliography* (Princeton: Princeton University Press, 1967), p. 9.

Chapter 4

1. As discussed earlier, pp. 65–66.

2. Carlos Baker, *Ernest Hemingway: A Life Story* (Princeton: Princeton University Press, 1969), p. 201. In his *Hemingway: The Writer as Artist* (Princeton: Princeton University Press, 1952), Baker declares, "There is a persistent tradition that the present ending was rewritten seventeen times before Hemingway got the corrected galley-proof aboard the boat-train," p. 97.

3. Philip Young and Charles W. Mann, *The Hemingway Manuscripts: An Inventory* (University Park: Pennsylvania State University Press, 1969), pp. 11–12. Item 5-F in this inventory describes a three-page manuscript ending in which the baby lives; Item 5-H mentions only that there are "Different versions of ending" attached to the foul galleys set for the *Scribner's Magazine* publication of the novel; and

Item 5-J merely adds that "four more endings of the novel" are attached to two galleys dated June 4, 1929. If this information seems somewhat vague, it should be said in fairness to Young and Mann that their inventory was meant to be an "interim report," as they declare in their preface, "and not the much more elaborate catalogue . . . that should be made when the papers have reached their permanent repository."

4. (New York: Scribner's, 1962), p. 75.

5. See Hemingway Collection, specifically Item 64 and Item 70: the first is the manuscript of the novel as first completed; the second is a series of drafts for an ending (some forty pages in manuscript and typescript). See also Michael Reynolds, *Hemingway's First War: The Making of "A Farewell to Arms"* (Princeton: Princeton University Press, 1976), pp. 46–48.

6. Item 64 and Item 70, as mentioned in note 5 above.

7. Used with a slightly contradictory connotation in the title of this chapter, this phrase is borrowed from Frank Kermode's challenging analysis of apocalyptic literary endings: *The Sense of an Ending: Studies in the Theory of Fiction* (New York: Oxford University Press, 1967).

8. *A Farewell to Arms,* Modern Standard Authors edition (New York: Scribner's, 1953), p. 343.

9. This variant has been published in Reynolds' study, p. 294.

10. See Philip Young and Charles W. Mann, "Fitzgerald's *Sun Also Rises:* Notes and Comment," *Fitzgerald/Hemingway Annual 1970* (Washington D.C.: NCR Microcard Editions, 1970), pp. 1–9. See also Item 77 of the Hemingway Collection, which contains Fitzgerald's comments on an early form of the novel, most probably Item 65, the original typescript and setting copy of *A Farewell to Arms.*

11. As reprinted in George Perkins' *The Theory of the American Novel* (New York: Holt, Rinehart and Winston, 1970), p. 334.

12. See note 5 and Reynolds, pp. 46–48.

13. There is a date established for Item 64, the manuscript copy of the novel (see note 14 below), but the great bulk of the variants, found in Item 70, are not dated.

14. See Reynolds, pp. 50, 285.

15. Kenneth Burke, *A Grammar of Motives* and *A Rhetoric of Motives,* a double-volume edition (Cleveland: World, 1962); this citation is from the second volume, p. 850.

16. As the author of this study recently discovered, there is another good reason for Hemingway's dropping this line: it is used by Fitz-

gerald in the last chapter of *The Great Gatsby,* in the funeral scene: "Dimly I heard someone murmur 'Blessed are the dead that the rain falls on,' and then the owl-eyed man said 'Amen to that' in a brave voice." Whether the line is original or not with Fitzgerald, Hemingway would have looked overly dependent in using it for similar effect in conclusion.

17. In George Plimpton's interview with the author, "Ernest Hemingway: The Art of Fiction XXI," *Paris Review* 18 (Spring 1958), p. 84.

18. E. M. Forster, *Aspects of the Novel* (1927; rpt. New York: Harcourt, Brace, 1954), p. 95.

19. Ibid., pp. 168–169.

20. As quoted by Frank Kermode in *The Sense of an Ending,* p. 174.

21. Ibid., p. 175.

22. Martin Heidegger, *Existence and Being* (Chicago: Regnery, 1960), p. 331; for other elements of Heidegger's discussion paraphrased and quoted here, see pp. 326–344.

23. Ibid., p. 345.

24. *A Rhetoric of Motives,* p. 851.

25. Most of the concluding attempts negate and reject; none gives any indication of "new intimacies." (See particularly the examples given on pp. 107–110.) The only sense in which Frederic Henry makes a new beginning is in telling his story about Catherine and himself.

26. Henry James, *Roderick Hudson* (1907; rpt. New York: Augustus M. Kelley, 1971), p. vii.

Index

Aldington, Richard, 7, 65, 117
Anderson, Charles, 114
Anderson, Sherwood, 31
Andreev, Leonid, 18
August, Jo [Curator of The Hemingway Collection, John F. Kennedy Library], x, 115

Bacon, Sir Francis, 53
Baker, Carlos, x, 2, 3, 26, 43, 58, 65, 71, 77, 105, 111, 112, 115, 117
Balzac, Honoré de, 38
Barbusse, Henri, 7
Barth, John, 89
Beardsley, Monroe C., 42, 114
Beauvoir, Simone de, 114
Beckett, Samuel, 84
Bildungsroman, 24, 37, 76
Blake, William, ix, 84
Book of Common Prayer, 12
Borges, Jorge Luis, ix, 39
Brooks, Cleanth, 111
Browning, Elizabeth Barrett, 20
Bunyan, John, 16, 25
Burke, Kenneth, 11, 80, 90, 112, 118

Camus, Albert, 84
Canby, Henry Seidel, 8, 111, 113
Caporetto, 21, 30, 32, 45, 47, 48, 115
Capote, Truman, 39
Cervantes, Miguel de, 33
Chamberlain, Neville, 12, 112
Churchill, Winston, 112
Conrad, Joseph, 75
Cowley, Malcolm, 2, 8, 10, 23, 31
Crabbe, George, 20
Crane, Stephen, 47

"Daemon Lover, The," 21
Dickens, Charles, 86
Donne, John, 13, 18
Dos Passos, John, 5
Dostoevsky, Fyodor, 85
Drummond, William ["Spring Bereaved"], 18

Ecclesiastes, 12
"Edward, Edward," 17
Eliot, George [Mary Ann Evans], 57, 83
Eliot, T. S., 12, 19, 22, 26, 29, 64, 84, 113
"ex nihilo nihil fit," 87
Existence and Being. See Heidegger

Fadiman, Clifton, 8
Faulkner, William, 12, 27, 38, 66, 86
Fiesta, 13
Fitzgerald, F. Scott, 2, 4, 5, 8, 9, 12, 27, 57, 59–61, 64, 73–75, 78, 82, 85, 101–102, 105, 107, 116, 118
Flaubert, Gustave, 18–19, 25, 38, 63, [*Madame Bovary*] 85, 116
Ford, Ford Madox, 2, 23, 62
Forster, E. M., 83, 90, 119
France, Anatole, 37
Frye, Northrop, 38

Galsworthy, John, 6, 111
Goethe, Johann Wolfgang von, 17
Graves, Robert, 31
Great Gatsby, The, 118
Greppi, Giuseppe Count, 45–47, 59